Principles of Sanctification

Principles of Sanctification

Charles G. Finney

Compiled & Edited by
Louis Gifford Parkhurst, Jr.

BETHANY HOUSE PUBLISHERS
MINNEAPOLIS, MINNESOTA 55438
A Division of Bethany Fellowship, Inc.
Gospel Truth
P.O. Box 6322
Orange, CA 92863

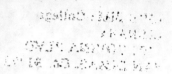

An expanded edition of Finney's *Views of Sanctification* first published in 1840. This new volume includes articles by two important professors who worked with Finney at Oberlin College: James H. Fairchild and Henry Cowles. A companion volume will include Finney's "Letters on Sanctification" from *The Oberlin Evangelist* and be titled *Principles of Discipleship*. Finney's "Letters on Revival" from *The Oberlin Evangelist* can be found in *Reflections on Revival*.

Published by Bethany House Publishers
A Division of Bethany Fellowship, Inc.
6820 Auto Club Road, Minneapolis, Minnesota 55438

Printed in the United States of America

Library of Congress Cataloging-in-Publication Data

Finney, Charles Grandison, 1792–1875.
    Principles of sanctification.

    Rev. ed. of: Finney's Views of sanctification. 1840.
    Includes appendix, Convention on entire sanctification and articles
by James H. Fairchild and Henry Cowles.
    1. Sanctification. I. Parkhurst, Louis Gifford, 1946–
II. Finney, Charles Grandison, 1792–1875.
Views of sanctification. III. Title.
BT765.F56   1986   234'.8   86–9664
ISBN 0–87123–859–4

CHARLES G. FINNEY was one of America's foremost evangelists. Over half a million people were converted under his ministry in an age that offered neither amplifiers nor mass communications as tools. Harvard Professor Perry Miller affirmed that "Finney led America out of the eighteenth century." As a theologian, he is best known for his *Revival Lectures* and his *Systematic Theology*.

LOUIS GIFFORD PARKHURST, JR., is pastor of First Christian Church of Rochester, Minnesota, and teaches Ethics/Philosophy at Minnesota Bible College. He garnered a B.A. and an M.A. from the University of Oklahoma and an M.Div. degree from Princeton Theological Seminary. He is married and the father of two children.

OTHER BOOKS IN THIS SERIES

OTHER BOOKS BY FINNEY

CONTENTS

INTRODUCTION

When Charles Finney arrived at Oberlin College as Professor of Theology, his early tent preaching sparked regular revivals, influencing both the college and the community. After almost everyone in Oberlin professed to be Christians, the residents—faculty and students—began to inquire about how to live the Christian life better. Hence, the question of the doctrine of sanctification arose.

All Christians should be familiar with three important doctrines: justification, sanctification, and glorification. *Justification* is that experience by which a person becomes a Christian by grace through faith in the finished work of Christ on the cross. We are justified through faith in the death of Jesus Christ as our substitute. To begin the Christian life of faith, we must accept God's free and unmerited gift of forgiveness. When we are justified, we can begin to live in a new relationship with God through Christ as His adopted children.

Sanctification has to do with living out the Christian life on this earth and throughout eternity. We are sanctified by the truth of God's Word and the indwelling Holy Spirit through faith. Sanctification means living a holy life of love in appreciation for being justified, a life that honors the Holy God who has loved and saved us. In philosophy the study of the doctrine of sanctification is reduced to the study of ethics or morality, of the concept of right and wrong, and of man's ability to choose and do what is right.

Glorification involves the physical death and bodily resurrection of those who are justified and sanctified. Someday, Christians will be given a glorified body, just as Jesus received a glorified human body when He was raised from the dead. Christians will experience glorification when Christ comes again. However, all Christians must know and experience justification and sanctification personally before they die.

Properly speaking, *salvation* for the individual involves the total process of justification, sanctification, and glorification. For this reason, three tenses are used to describe salvation: "I have been saved, I am being saved, and I will be saved." Each tense corresponds to the three concepts we have discussed above respectively.

Principles of Sanctification deals with the important concept of what it means to live in a proper relationship with God the Father, Son and Holy Spirit, after being justified. The question about the meaning and extent of personal sanctification in this life was raised among the serious faculty and students at Oberlin College about the year 1836. The newspaper, *The Oberlin Evangelist*, began publication in 1839 to discuss this important matter. Articles and sermons supporting the differing views of the faculty, as well as contrary opinions, were published in an open forum for the public to evaluate. Today, *The Oberlin Evangelist* is an important resource for the study of the growth and development of the doctrine of sanctification at Oberlin among her professors and students.

In a sense, this book is a part of a series within a series. It is the eighth title in the *Principles* series, but it also falls within a series of Finney's books on *sanctification*. This book is the first of three projected volumes on the important question of sanctification.

Timothy Smith compiled and edited the first volume of new Finney titles on sanctification with *The Promise of the Spirit*. That work includes Finney's sermons and letters from the first volume of *The Oberlin Evangelist* published through the end of 1839.

With his first lecture published in *The Oberlin Evangelist* in 1840, Finney began a series of nine lectures specifically on the doctrine of sanctification. Almost immediately, in 1840, these lectures were published in one long continuous chapter as a book, *Views of Sanctification*. Throughout the rest of 1840, Finney published letters to ministers, parents, and others in *The Oberlin Evangelist*. *Principles of Sanctification* contains the nine lectures divided into twelve chapters. Another book, *Principles of Discipleship*, will include all of Finney's letters from 1840.

Following these lectures, Finney published many sermons in *The Oberlin Evangelist* through the years 1841–1842. In these sermons Finney applied the doctrine of sanctification specifically to laymen. These sermons will be published as the third new title in the series on sanctification as *Principles of Christian Obedience*.

In 1843 Finney preached yet another series of sermons on sanctification titled, "Holiness of Christians in the Present Life." These sermons were included in the book *Principles of Holiness*.

Throughout the following years of Finney's preaching, students who attended Oberlin listened attentively for a sermon on sanctification, and they complained that they heard none. But those who were quite familiar with the Oberlin teachings on the subject said they heard one every week. For this reason, it has become increasingly clear to me that most of Finney's sermons in *Principles of Victory* and *Principles of Liberty* are also sermons on sanctification.

Principles of Union with Christ describes the important relationship each person must have with Christ in order to overcome sin and temptation. Taken from Finney's *Lectures on Systematic Theology*, the 1851 edition, chronologically it represents the last book in the series on sanctification currently available. Finney's biographer, G. F. Wright, said of the ideas in *Principles of Union with Christ*: "With Mr. Finney, sanctification is really *confirmation* or *stability* of will—a state to be secured by the enlightening of the Holy Spirit in revealing Christ to the soul. The practical effect of his discussion, when understood, is to enhance one's sense of the enormity of present sin, rather than to beget a presumptuous confidence of future security, and least of all is it calculated to encourage boasting in the flesh. The two hundred pages [*Systematic Theology*, pp. 568–766] which President Finney has devoted to the offices of Christ in securing our sanctification will always remain a classic of devotional literature, and wherever known will be best appreciated by the most devout in the Christian church."[1]

As you will discover from reading the article by President Fairchild in this book, important factors should be noted as we study the development of the doctrine of sanctification in Finney's thought and published works. First, the idea of the simplicity (or unity) of moral action was not completely developed and promoted at Oberlin until 1841. Although Fairchild believed that Finney adopted this view (explained thoroughly in *Finney's Systematic Theology*) in 1841, Finney actually preached from this perspective much earlier as his sermons indicate. *The Promise of the Spirit* and *Principles of Sanctification* expound Finney's views from the perspective of the doctrine of the simplicity of moral action. *Principles of Christian Obedience* will be sermons he preached as he was improving his presentation of the simplicity of moral action in its relation to sanctification, and *Principles of Holiness* contain his sermons after that doctrine was fully developed in its application.

Second, Fairchild points out, as you will discover in this book, that Finney used the terms entire consecration and entire sanctification interchangeably. This caused some confusion. Finney, however, wanted to use Bible names for Bible things, and so he emphasized the use of the names *sanctification* and *perfection* for entire consecration.

From the beginning of his work, Finney was criticized for his views. Many of the criticisms were unjustifiable for they were either based upon misreading, misunderstanding, or failing to read him at all. Finney guarded against perfectionism in the negative sense of that word very carefully, as you will note in this book. Yet, he promoted perfectionism in its best sense, and there are many rich and practical gems to be mined

---

[1]George F. Wright, "President Finney's System of Theology in Its Relations to the So-called New England Theology," *Bibliotheca Sacra*, October, 1877, pp. 734–735.

from the following pages. Many of his critics rebelled simply because he used the good biblical term "perfection"; they defined it in the negative sense and correspondingly read him with this prejudice. An astounding misrepresentation of Finney's views, handed down for over a hundred years and believed by many, is reprinted in full with Finney's "Letter of Reply" in *Principles of Discipleship.*

Third, Finney was criticized because his definition of total depravity differed from his hyper-Calvinistic critics. Finney distinguished between physical and moral depravity, even though he held to the doctrine of total depravity. His views in this regard are expounded fully in his *Systematic Theology.*[2] The article in this book by Henry Cowles will show how the doctrine of total depravity influenced the Reformers and those who tried to follow them in their views on sanctification. From the article by Cowles we can understand the conflict better in its historical context as seen by the professors at Oberlin.

In preparing this book for the press, I am indebted to several individuals and institutions. My thanks to an energetic and informed student of Finney's works, Mr. Tom Lukashow, for the use of a copy of the 1840 first edition of Finney's *Views of Sanctification,* published in Oberlin by James Steele. Thanks also goes to Mrs. Ardis Sawyer, Librarian of the Minnesota Bible College, who worked diligently to find me a copy of *Views of Sanctification,* and who found an available copy from the Moody Bible Institute: published in Toronto by the Toronto Willard Tract Depository in 1877. The endorsements from that edition are included in the Appendix. I am highly indebted, once again, to the Rev. Gordon C. Olson for giving me a copy of the article by Fairchild and suggesting that I publish it as a part of this volume. I also wish to thank Mr. Jack D. Key, Librarian of Mayo Clinic, for the use of his facilities in the reproduction of the needed materials from *The Oberlin Evangelist.* Finally, and most importantly, I wish to thank the editors and publisher of Bethany House Publishers for their continued interest in and support of this series. Their commitment to the truth, to Chris-

---

[2]Charles G. Finney, *Finney's Systematic Theology* (Minneapolis: Bethany House Publishers, 1976 reprint).

tian holiness, and to the spread of the gospel around the world should be highly commended in our day.

For the sake of His Kingdom,
L. G. Parkhurst, Jr.
January 23, 1985

1

WHAT IS SANCTIFICATION?

"And the very God of peace sanctify you wholly; and I pray God your whole spirit and soul and body be preserved blameless unto the coming of our Lord Jesus Christ. Faithful is he that calleth you, who also will do it" (1 Thess. 5:23, 24).

Define the term sanctification.

A definition of terms in all discussions is of prime importance. This is especially true of this subject. I have observed, almost without exception, that those who have written against the views presented here do so because they understand and define the terms, *sanctification* and *Christian perfection*, differently from the way I do. Everyone gives his own definition varying significantly from others and from what we understand by the terms. And then some go on openly opposing our teaching on sanctification, as though we taught it according to their definition. Now this is not only utterly unfair, but rather absurd. If I oppose a doctrine taught by another man, I am bound to oppose what he really holds. If I misrepresent his opinions, "I fight as one who beats the air."

I have been amazed at the different definitions that have been given to the terms *Christian perfection* and *sanctification*. There is such a diversity of opinion regarding what is and what is not implied in these terms! Some object wholly to the use of the term *Christian perfection*, because in their estimation it implies a number of things, which in my judgment are not implied at all. Some object to our use of the term *sanctification*, because that implies, according to their understanding of it, certain things that render its usage improper.

It is not my purpose to dispute about the use of words. I must, however, use some terms. I ought to be allowed to use Bible language in its Scriptural sense as I understand it. And if I sufficiently explain my meaning and define the sense in which I use the terms, this ought to suffice. I ask that nothing more nor less be understood by the language I use than what I profess to mean by it. Others may, if they please, use the same terms and give a different definition of them. But I have a right to hope and expect, if some feel called upon to oppose what I say, that they will bear in mind my definitions of the terms. I hope they will not pretend, as some have done, to oppose my views while they have only differed from me in their definition of the terms used. Some give their own definitions which vary considerably from the sense in which I use the same terms. They then array their arguments to prove that according to their definition, *sanctification* is not really attainable in this life. No one here or anywhere else, that I have ever heard of, has asserted that in their definition of the term, *sanctification* ever was or ever will be attainable in this life. And I might add, in that life which is to come.

Sanctification is a term frequently used in the Bible. Its simple and primary meaning is a state of consecration to God. To sanctify is to set apart to a holy use—to consecrate a thing to the service of God. A state of sanctification is a state of consecration, or being set apart to the service of God. This is plainly seen both in the Old and New Testament use of the term.

What is entire sanctification?

By *entire sanctification*, I mean the consecration of the whole being to God. In other words, it is that state of devotion to God and His service required by the moral law. The law is perfect. It requires just what is right, all that is right, and nothing more. Nothing more or less can possibly be *perfection* or *entire sanc-*

tification than obedience to the law. Obedience to the law of God, in an infant, a man, an angel, and in God himself, is perfection in each of them. Sanctification cannot possibly be anything above obedience to the law of God.

What is the distinction between entire and permanent sanctification?

A thing or a person may be for the time being wholly consecrated to God, and afterward desecrated or diverted from that service. Adam and "the angels who kept not their first estate" clearly demonstrate this. They were entirely sanctified and yet not permanently so.

By permanent sanctification I mean, then, a state not only of entire but of perpetual unending consecration to God.

What is not implied in entire sanctification?

The law of God is the only standard by which the question regarding what *is not* and what *is* implied in *entire sanctification* is to be decided. It is therefore extremely important that we understand what is and what is not implied in entire obedience to this law. It must be apparent to all that this inquiry is of prime importance. And to settle this question is one of the main goals of this discussion. The doctrine of entire sanctification of believers in this life can never be satisfactorily settled until it is clearly understood. And it cannot be understood until one knows what it does and what it does not imply. Our judgment of our own state or of the state of others can never be trusted until these questions are settled. In the present, vague, unsettled views of the Church on this question, nothing is more clear than this: no individual could claim to have attained this state without being a stumbling block to the Church.

Christ was perfect, and yet so erroneous were the notions of the Jews regarding what constituted perfection, they thought He was possessed with a devil, instead of being holy as He claimed to be. In our day, it would be impossible for a person to profess this state without being a stumbling block to himself and to others, unless all clearly understood what constitutes perfection. I will state, then, what is not implied in a state of entire sanctification, as I understand the law of God. The law is epitomized by Christ, "Thou shalt love the Lord thy God with all thy heart, and with all thy soul, and with all thy strength, and with all thy mind; and thy neighbor as thyself" (Luke 10:27). Here Christ proclaims the whole duty of man to God and to his fellow creatures. Now, let us consider what is not, and what is implied in perfect obedience to this law.

Vague notions regarding these questions have caused much error on the subject of entire sanctification. To settle these questions, a clear understanding of the rules of legal interpretation of the law is necessary. In the light of these, I believe the following list of rules will help to settle such questions:

Rule 1. Whatever is inconsistent with natural justice is not and cannot be law.

Rule 2. Whatever is inconsistent with the nature and relations of moral beings is contrary to natural justice and, therefore, cannot be law.

Rule 3. That which requires more than man has natural ability to perform is inconsistent with his nature and relations and, therefore, is inconsistent with natural justice, and of course is not law.

Rule 4. Law, then, must always be so understood and interpreted as to be consistent with the nature of the subjects, and with their relations to each other and to the lawgiver. Any interpretation that makes the law require more or less than is consistent with the nature and relations of moral beings is a virtual setting aside of law. Such a requirement actually nullifies itself as a law. No authority in heaven or on earth can make law, or place obligation upon moral agents, something which is inconsistent with their nature and relations.

Rule 5. Law must always be interpreted so as to cover the whole ground of natural right or justice. It must be clearly understood and explained so as to require all that is right in itself, and therefore immutably and unalterably right. Whatever professes to be law and does not fulfill this requirement is not and cannot be law.

Rule 6. Law must be so interpreted as not to require anything *more* than is consistent with natural justice or with the nature and relations of moral beings. If this requirement is not met, it is not law.

Rule 7. Laws are never to be interpreted so as to imply the possession of any attributes or strength and perfection of attributes which the subject does not possess.

Take for illustration the second commandment, "Thou shalt love thy neighbor as thyself." The simple meaning of this commandment seems to be that we are to regard and treat every person and interest according to its relative value. Now we are not to understand this commandment as expressly or impliedly requiring us to *know* the exact relative value of every person and thing in the universe in all cases. This would imply that we possess the attribute of omniscience. No mind short of an omniscient one can have this knowledge. The commandment, then, requires us to judge with candor the relative value of different interests, and treat them according to their value, so far as we understand it. I repeat the rule. Laws must never be interpreted to imply the possession of any attribute or strength and perfection of attributes which the subject does not possess.

Rule 8. Law is never to be interpreted to require that which is naturally impossible on account of our circumstances. "Thou shalt love the Lord thy God with all thy heart, etc.," is not to be interpreted so as to require us to make God the constant and sole object of attention, thought and affection, for this would not only be plainly impossible in our circumstances but obviously contrary to duty.

Rule 9. Law is never to be interpreted to make one requirement inconsistent with another. For example, if the first commandment is interpreted to mean that we are required to make God the only object of thought, attention and affection, then we cannot obey the second commandment, which requires us to love our neighbor. And if the first commandment is interpreted to mean that every faculty and power must be directed solely to the comtemplation and love of God, then love to all other beings is prohibited and the second commandment is set aside. I repeat the rule therefore: laws are not to be interpreted so that they conflict with each other.

Rule 10. A law requiring perpetual benevolence must be interpreted so as to agree with, and require all the appropriate and necessary modifications of, the following principles under various circumstances: justice, mercy, anger at sin and sinners, and a special and admiring regard to those who are virtuous.

Rule 11. Law must be interpreted so that its claims apply only to the voluntary faculties. To attempt to legislate over the involuntary faculties would contradict natural justice. You may as well attempt to legislate over the beatings of the heart as over any involuntary mental actions.

Rule 12. In morals, actual knowledge is indispensable to obligation. The maxim *ignorantia legis non excusat*—"ignorance of the law excuses no one," is applicable to the realm of moral action only to a very limited degree. The following Scriptures clearly show that actual knowledge is indispensable to moral obligation: "Therefore to him that knoweth to do good, and doeth it not, to him it is sin" (James 4:17). "And that servant, which knew his lord's will, and prepared not himself, neither did according to his will, shall be beaten with many stripes. But he that knew not, and did commit things worthy of stripes, shall be beaten with few stripes. For unto whomsoever much is given, of him shall be much required: and to whom men have committed much, of him they will ask the more" (Luke 12:47, 48). "Jesus said unto them, If ye were blind, ye should have no sin: but now ye say, We see; therefore your sin remaineth" (John 9:41). In Romans one and two the Apostle argues at length on this subject. Paul convicts the heathen of sin on the grounds that they violate their own conscience, and do not live according to the truth they have.

This principle is recognized throughout the Bible: an increase of knowledge increases obligation. The Scriptures plainly recognize that knowledge is indispensable to and equal with obligation. In sins of ignorance, the sin lies in the ignorance itself, but not in the neglect of what is unknown. A man may be guilty of present or past neglect to ascertain the truth. Here his ignorance is sin. The heathen are guilty for not living up to the light of nature, but are under no obligation to embrace Christianity until they have had the opportunity to do so.

Rule 13. Moral laws must be interpreted consistently with physical laws. In other words, the application of the moral law to human beings must recognize man as he is, as both a physical and intellectual being. Moral law must be interpreted this way so that obedience to it will not violate the laws of the physical constitution and cause premature destruction of the body.

Rule 14. Law must be interpreted to recognize all the attributes and circumstances of both body and soul. In the application of the law of God to human beings, we are to regard a person's faculties and attributes as they really are, and not as they are not.

Rule 15. Law must be interpreted as an obligation over *actions*, and not be extended to the *nature* or *constitution* of moral beings. Moral law must not be understood to extend its legislation over man's nature, or to require a man to possess certain attributes. Moral law prescribes a rule of action. The law does not require the existence or possession of certain attributes, or that these attributes should exist in a certain state of perfection. The law requires the right use of all these attributes as they are.

Rule 16. The obedience of the heart to any law implies and includes faith or confidence in the lawgiver. But no law should be interpreted so as to require faith in what the intellect does not perceive. A man may be under obligation to understand what he does not; that is, it may be his duty to inquire after and ascertain the truth. But until the intellect obtains a perception of the things to be believed, obligation to believe with the heart does not apply.

In light of these rules, we will now proceed to inquire in the next two chapters concerning: (1) *What is not*, and (2) *What is implied* in perfect obedience to the law of God, or in *entire sanctification*.

2

WHAT ENTIRE SANCTIFICATION IS NOT

According to the rules in the previous chapter, let us now consider what is *not* implied in perfect obedience to the law of God or in *entire sanctification*.

1. Entire sanctification does not imply any change in the substance of the soul or body. The law does not require this. If it did, it would not be obligatory, because the requirement would be inconsistent with natural justice. *Entire sanctification is the entire consecration of the faculties, as they are, to God. It does not imply any change in the faculties themselves, but simply the right use of them.*

2. Entire sanctification does not imply any annihilation of constitutional traits of character, such as natural zeal or impulsiveness. There is nothing in the law of God that requires such constitutional traits to be annihilated. They simply should be rightly directed.

3. Entire sanctification does not imply the annihilation of any of the innate desires or feelings. Some suppose that the innate appetites and feelings are in themselves sinful, and that a state of entire sanctification would imply their total annihilation. And I have often been astonished at the fact that those who oppose the doctrine of entire sanctification in this life assume the sinfulness of man's basic nature. I have been greatly surprised to find that some persons, who I had supposed were far from embracing the doctrine of physical depravity, were, after all, resorting to this assumption in order to set aside the

doctrine of entire sanctification in this life.

Let us appeal to the law. Does the law condemn the constitution of man or require the annihilation of anything that is properly a part of his constitution itself? Does the law require the annihilation of the appetite for food, or is it satisfied merely with regulating its indulgence? In short, does the law of God anywhere require anything more than the consecration of all the appetites and feelings of the body and mind to the service of God?

At one time, a brother insisted to me that a man might perpetually obey the law of God and be guilty of no actual transgression, and yet not be entirely sanctified. He insisted that there might be something in him which would lay the foundation for his sinning at a future time. When questioned with regard to what that something in him was, he replied, "that which first led him to sin at the beginning of his moral existence." I answered that that which first led him to sin was his innocent nature, just as it was the innocent nature of Adam to which the temptation was addressed that led him into sin. Adam's innocent innate desires when excited by the presence of objects fitted to excite them, were a sufficient temptation to lead him to consent to a forbidden indulgence, which constituted sin. It certainly is the same with every human being today. The constitution, the substance of a person's body and soul, certainly cannot have any moral character. But when these desires, which are essential to his nature and have no moral character in themselves, are excited, they lead to forbidden indulgence. In this way, every human being is led into sin.

Now, if a man cannot be entirely sanctified until that which first *occasioned* his sin is annihilated, then it seems that as long as he possesses either body or soul he can never be entirely sanctified. I insist, therefore, that entire sanctification does not imply the annihilation of any innate desire or feeling, but only the entire consecration of the whole constitution as it is, to the service of God.

4. Entire sanctification does not imply the annihilation of natural affection or resentment. By natural affection, I mean that certain persons may be naturally pleasing to us. Christ

appears to have had a natural affection for John. By natural resentment, I mean that from the laws of our being we must resent or feel opposed to such things as injustice or ill treatment. I do not mean that a disposition to retaliate or revenge ourselves is consistent with the law of God. Perfect obedience to the law of God does not imply that we should not feel injury and injustice when we are abused. God has this sense of injustice, and rightly so, as does every other moral being. To love your neighbor as yourself does not imply that if he should injure you, you should feel no sense of the injury or injustice. The law requires that you love him and do him good, in spite of his ill treatment of you.

5. Entire sanctification does not imply any unhealthy degree of excitement of mind. Rule Thirteen states that moral law is to be interpreted so as to be consistent with physical law. God's laws certainly do not clash with each other. The moral law cannot require such a state of constant mental excitement as to destroy the physical constitution. The moral law cannot require any more mental excitement and action than is consistent with all the laws, attributes, and circumstances of both soul and body, as stated in Rule Fourteen.

6. Entire sanctification does not imply that any organ or faculty is to be exerted at all times to its full strength. This would soon exhaust and destroy any and every organ of the body. Whatever may be true of the mind when separated from the body, it is certain that while it acts through a material organ a constant state of excitement is impossible. When the mind is strongly excited, out of necessity there is a great flow of blood to the brain. A high degree of excitement certainly cannot continue long without producing inflammation of the brain and consequent insanity. The law of God does not require any degree of emotion or mental excitement that is inconsistent with life and health. Our Lord Jesus Christ does not appear to have been in a state of *continual* excitement. When He and His disciples had experienced a time of great excitement, they would turn aside "and rest awhile."

Therefore, it is obvious that the high degree of excitement which is sometimes witnessed in revivals of religion must necessarily be short, or the people will become deranged. It seems indispensable sometimes that a high degree of excitement should prevail for a time in order to attract public and individual attention, and to draw people away from other pursuits in order to attend to the needs of their souls. But if any suppose that this high degree of excitement is either necessary, or desirable, or possible to be continued for long, they have not wisely considered the matter. And this is a great mistake of the Church. She has supposed that revival consists mostly of a state of excited emotion rather than the conformity of the human will to the will of God. Hence, when the reasons for much excitement have ceased, and the public mind begins to grow more calm, they immediately begin to say that the revival is on the decline; when, in actual fact, with much less excited emotion, there may be a great deal more of actual religion in the community.

Excitement is often important and indispensable. But the vigorous acts of the will are infinitely more important. And this state of mind may exist in the absence of highly excited emotions.

7. Entire sanctification does not imply that the same degree of emotion, volition, or intellectual effort be required at all times. All volitions do not require the same strength. They cannot have equal strength because they are not produced by equally powerful reasons. Should a man exercise as strong a volition to pick up an apple as he would to extinguish the flames of a burning house? Should a mother, when watching over her sleeping baby while all is quiet and secure, exercise the same volitions that would be required to snatch him from devouring flames? Now, suppose that she was equally devoted to God in watching over her sleeping baby and in rescuing him from the jaws of death. Her holiness would not lie in the fact that she exercised equally strong volitions in both cases; but, that in both cases, the volition was equal to the accomplishment of the thing required. So, people may be entirely holy, and yet continually varying in the strength of their affections according to their circumstances, the state of their physical system, and the business in which they are engaged.

All the powers of body and mind are to be held at the service and disposal of God. Appropriate physical, intellectual, and moral energy are to be expended in the performance of duty as the nature and the circumstances of the case require. The law of God does not require a constant intense state of emotion and mental action on any and every subject alike.

8. Entire sanctification does not imply, as I have said, that God is at all times to be the direct object of attention and affection. This is not only impossible in the nature of the case, but would render it impossible for us to love our neighbor or ourselves: Rule Nine.

I have formerly explained this subject with the following language: the law of God requires the supreme love of the heart. By this I mean the mind's supreme preference should be God, and God should be the great object of supreme love and delight. This state of mind is perfectly consistent with our involvement in any of the necessary activities of life, of giving attention to business, and of exercising all those affections and emotions which its nature and importance demand.

If a man loves God supremely and engages in any business for the promotion of His glory, if his eye is single, then his affections and conduct are entirely holy. When a man necessarily engages in the right *transaction* of his business, although for the time being neither his thoughts or affections are on God, his conduct is holy.

A man who is supremely devoted to his family may be acting consistently with his supreme affection, rendering them the most important and perfect service, while he does not think of them at all. It is my firm conviction that the moral heart of a man lies in the mind's supreme preference. Correspondingly, the natural or fleshly heart is the seat of bodily life, and propels the blood through all the physical system. Now, there is a striking analogy between this and the moral heart. And the analogy consists in this: as the natural heart, by its pulsations diffuses life through the physical system; so the moral heart, or the supreme governing preference of the mind, gives life and character to man's moral actions. Suppose that I teach mathematics, and that the supreme desire of my mind is to glorify God in this particular calling. In demonstrating some of its intricate propositions, I am obliged to give the entire attention of my mind to that object for hours. Now, while my mind is so intensely occupied with mathematics, it is impossible that I should have any thoughts directly about God, or should exercise any direct affections or emotions or volitions toward God. Yet, if in this particular calling all selfishness is excluded and my supreme design is to glorify God, then my mind is in a sanctified state, even though for the time being I do not think of God.

When the supreme preference of the mind excludes all selfishness, and exercises the appropriate strength of volition, thought, affection, and emotion that is required to rightly carry out any duty to which the mind may be called, the heart is in a sanctified state. By a suitable degree of thought and feeling to the right discharge of duty, I mean the necessary intensity of thought and energy of action that the nature and importance of the particular duty at hand demands. In this statement, I take it for granted that the brain, together with all the circumstances of the constitution, is such that the required amount of thought, feeling, etc., is possible. If the physical body is in a state of exhaustion and unable to exercise that amount of exertion which the nature of the subject might otherwise demand, then the feeble efforts, though far below the importance of the subject, would be all that the law of God requires. Whoever supposes that a state of entire sanctification implies a state of entire abstraction of mind from everything but God labors under a grievous mistake. Such a state of mind is as inconsistent with duty as it is impossible while we are in the flesh.

The language and spirit of the law in the past and even now generally are grossly misunderstood and misinterpreted to mean what they never did or can mean consistently with natural justice. Many minds have been thrown open to the assaults of Satan and kept in a state of continual bondage and condemnation. This is because they believed that God was to be the sole object of thought, affection and emotion at all times, and that the mind needed to be kept in a state of perfect tension and great excitement at every moment.

9. Entire sanctification does not imply a state of continual calmness of mind. Christ did not experience a state of continual

calmness. While the deep peace of His mind remained undisturbed, the surface or emotions of His mind were often in a state of great excitement.

Here, let me refer to Christ, as we have His history in the Bible, to illustrate the positions I have already taken. Christ had all the normal desires and feelings of human nature. Had it been otherwise, He could not have been "tempted in all points like as we are." He possessed a constitution similar to our own. Christ also manifested natural affection for His mother, and for other friends. He showed that He had a sense of injury and injustice. He exercised an appropriate resentment when He was injured and persecuted. He was not always in a state of great excitement. He appears to have had His seasons of excitement and of calm—of labor and rest—of joy and sorrow, like other good men. Some have spoken of entire sanctification as implying a state of uniform and universal calmness, as if every kind and degree of excited feeling were inconsistent with this state, except when the feelings of love toward God are excited. But Christ often manifested a great degree of excitement when reproving the enemies of God. In short, His history would lead to the conclusion that His calmness and excitement varied, according to the circumstances of the case. And although He was sometimes very pointed and severe in His reproof, as to be accused of being possessed by a devil, yet His emotions and feelings were only those that were called for and suited to the occasions.

10. Entire sanctification does not imply a state of continual tranquility of mind without any indignation or holy anger at sin or sinners. Anger at sin is only a modification of love. A feeling of justice, or a desire to have the wicked punished for the benefit of the government, is only another of the modifications of love. Such feelings are essential to the existence of love, where the circumstances call for their exercise. The Bible mentions when Christ was angry. He often manifested anger and holy indignation. "God is angry with the wicked every day" (Ps. 7:11). Holiness, or a state of sanctification, always implies the existence of anger when the circumstances demand it: Rule Ten.

11. Entire sanctification does not imply a state of mind full of compassion with no feeling of justice. Compassion is only one of the modifications of love. Justice, or a desire for the execution of law and the punishment of sin, is another of its modifications. God, and Christ, and all holy beings exercise all those affections and emotions that constitute the different modifications of love under every possible circumstance.

12. Entire sanctification does not imply that we should love or hate all men alike, irrespective of their value, circumstances, and relations. One being may have a greater capacity for happiness and as a result be of much more importance to the universe than another. Impartiality and the law of love require us not to regard all beings and things alike; but rather according to their nature, relations and circumstances.

13. Nor does entire sanctification imply a perfect knowledge of all our relations: Rule Seven. An interpretation of the law that would make it necessary for us to understand all our relations in order to obey it would imply that we possess the attribute of omniscience. Certainly there is not a thing in the universe to which we do not sustain some relation. A knowledge of all these relations plainly implies infinite knowledge. The law of God cannot require this; therefore, entire sanctification or entire obedience to the law of God implies no such thing.

14. Nor does entire sanctification imply perfect knowledge on any subject. Perfect knowledge on any subject implies a perfect knowledge of its nature, relations, influences, and tendencies. Since every single thing in the universe sustains some relation to and has some influence on every other thing, there can be no such thing as perfect knowledge on any one subject that does not embrace universal or infinite knowledge.

15. Nor does entire sanctification imply freedom from mistake on any subject whatever. Some maintain that the grace of the gospel pledges to every man perfect knowledge, or at least such knowledge as to exempt him from any mistake. Without discussing this at length, I would like to clarify that the law of God does not expressly or impliedly require infallibility of judgment in us. It only requires us to make the best of all the truth we have.

16. Nor does entire sanctification imply the knowledge of the exact relative value of different interests. I have already said, in illustrating Rule Seven, that the second commandment, "Thou shalt love thy neighbor as thyself," does not imply that we should, in every instance, understand exactly the relative value and importance of every interest. This plainly cannot be required, unless it is assumed that we are omniscient.

17. Entire sanctification does not imply the same degree of knowledge that we might have acquired if we had rightly used our time in its acquisition. The law cannot require us to love God or man as well as we might have been able to love them had we always rightly used all our time in obtaining all the knowledge we could have in regard to their nature, character, and interests. If this were implied in the demands of the law, there is not a saint on earth or in heaven that is or ever can be perfect. What is lost in this respect is lost, and past neglect can never be so atoned for so that we will ever be able to make up in our acquisitions of knowledge what we have lost. It will no doubt be true throughout all eternity that we shall have less knowledge than we might have possessed, had we diligently used all our time in acquiring it. We do not, cannot, nor will we ever, be able to love God as well as we might have loved Him had we always applied our minds to acquiring knowledge concerning Him. If entire sanctification is to be understood to imply that we love God as much as we could, had we all the knowledge we might have acquired, then I repeat it; there is not a saint on earth or in heaven, nor ever will be, that is entirely sanctified.

18. Entire sanctification does not require the same amount of service that we might have rendered had we never sinned. The law of God does not imply or suppose that our faculties are in a perfect state. Our strength of body or mind is not what it would have been had we never sinned. The law of God simply requires us to use what strength we do have. The very wording of the law is conclusive proof that it extends its demands only to the full amount of what strength we have. This is true of every moral being however great or small.

19. Entire sanctification does not require the same degree

of love that we might have rendered if it was not for our ignorance. We certainly know much less of God, and therefore are much less capable of loving Him and to a lesser degree, than if we knew more of Him, which we might have done if it was not for our sins. And as I have said before, this will be true throughout all eternity. We can never make amends by any future obedience or diligence for this problem any more than for other sins. It will remain true throughout all eternity that we will know less of God, and love Him less than we might and should have done, had we always done our duty. If entire sanctification implies the same degree of love or service that might have been rendered had we always developed our faculties by a perfect use of them, then there is not a saint on earth or in heaven that experiences or ever will experience that state. The most perfect development and improvement of our faculties must depend on their most perfect use. And every departure from their perfect use is a diminishing of their highest development, and a curtailing of their capabilities to serve God in the highest and best manner. All sin, then, cripples and curtails the faculties of body and mind and renders them, by just that much, incapable of performing the service they might otherwise have rendered.

In view of this subject, some have objected that Christ taught an opposite doctrine, in the case of the woman who washed His feet with her tears, when He said, "To whom much is forgiven, the same loveth much." But can it be that Christ intended us to understand that to mean the more we sin the greater our love and our ultimate virtue will be? If this is so I do not see why it does not logically follow that the more sin in this life, the better, if we are forgiven. If our virtue is really improved by our sins, I see not why it would not be profitable both for God and man to sin as much as we can while in this world. Christ certainly did not mean to lay down such a principle as this. He undoubtedly meant to teach that a person who was truly aware of the greatness of his sins would exercise more of the *love of gratitude* than one who was less conscious of the punishment he deserved.

20. Entire sanctification does not imply the same degree of faith that might have been exercised if it had not been for our ignorance and past sin.

We cannot believe anything about God of which we have no evidence or knowledge. Our faith, therefore, must be limited by our intellectual perceptions of truth. The heathen are not under obligation to believe in Christ, and thousands of other things of which they have no knowledge. Perfection in a heathen would imply much less faith than in a Christian. Perfection in an adult would imply much more and greater faith than in an infant. And perfection in an angel would imply much greater faith than in a man, exactly in proportion as he knows more of God than man. *Let it always be understood that entire sanctification never implies that which is naturally impossible.* It is naturally impossible for us to believe something of which we have no knowledge. Entire sanctification, in this respect, implies nothing more than the heart's faith or confidence in all the truth that is perceived by the intellect.

21. Nor does entire sanctification imply the conversion of all men in answer to our prayers. Some maintain that a state of entire sanctification implies the offering of prevailing prayer for the conversion of all men. To this I reply:

a. Then Christ was not sanctified, for He offered no such prayer.

b. The law of God makes no such demand either expressly or impliedly.

c. We have no right to believe that all men will be converted in answer to our prayers, unless we have an express promise to that effect.

d. Therefore, since there is no such promise, we are under no obligation to offer such prayer. Nor does the non-conversion of the world imply that there are no sanctified saints in the world.

22. Entire sanctification does not imply the conversion of anyone for whom there is not an express or implied promise in the Word of God. The fact that Christ did not pray in faith for the conversion of Judas, and that Judas was not converted in answer to His prayers, does not prove that Christ was not in a state of entire sanctification.

23. Nor does entire sanctification imply that all those things which are expressly or impliedly promised will be granted in

answer to our prayers. In other words, it does not mean that we should pray in faith for them if we are ignorant of the existence or application of those promises. *A state of perfect love implies the discharge of known duty.* And strictly speaking, nothing can be duty of which the mind has no knowledge. It cannot be our duty to believe a promise of which we are entirely ignorant, or to apply what we do not understand about it to any specific object.

If any sin exists in such a case as this, it lies in the ignorance itself. And here, no doubt, there often is sin, because there is present neglect to know the truth. But it should always be understood that the sin lies in the ignorance, and not in the neglect of that of which we have no knowledge. *A state of sanctification is inconsistent with any present neglect to know the truth; for such neglect is sin.* But it is not inconsistent with our failing to do that of which we have no knowledge. James says: "To him that knoweth to do good, and doeth it not, to him it is sin" (James 4:17). "If ye were blind," says Christ, "ye should have no sin; but now ye say, We see; therefore your sin remaineth" (John 9:41).

24. *Entire sanctification does not imply the impossibility of future sin.* Entire and *permanent* sanctification does imply the fact that the sanctified soul *will* not sin. The only reason why he will not sin is entirely due to the sovereign grace of God. Sanctification does not imply, as I have already said, any such change in the nature of the subject as to render it impossible or improbable that he will sin again. I do not suppose there is a man on earth, or perhaps in heaven, who would not fall into sin if it weren't for the supporting grace of God.

25. Entire sanctification does not imply that watchfulness, prayer, and effort are no longer needed. It is unreasonable to suppose that either in this or any other state of being, there will be no need for faith or watchfulness against temptation. As long as the susceptibilities of our souls exist, temptation in some sense and to some extent must exist in whatever world we live. Christ manifestly struggled hard with temptation. He found watchfulness, the most powerful opposition to temptation, indispensable to His perseverance in holiness. "Is the ser-

vant above his master, or the disciple above his Lord?"

26. Nor does entire sanctification imply that we are no longer dependent on the grace of Christ. Rather, the exact opposite is implied. A state of entire and permanent sanctification implies the most constant and perfect reliance upon the grace and strength of an indwelling Christ. It seems that some have supposed that entire sanctification implies that something has been done to change the nature of the sanctified soul so that from then on he will persevere in holiness in his own strength. This idea is totally inconsistent with the truth. *No change whatever had occurred in the nature of the individual, except that he has learned to confide simply in Christ at every step. He has so received Christ's strength as to lean constantly upon His supporting grace**.

27. Nor does entire sanctification imply that the Christian warfare is ended. I understand the Christian warfare to consist in the mind's conflict with temptation. This certainly will never end in this life.

28. Nor does entire sanctification imply that there is no more growth in grace. Many persons seem to understand the command "Grow in grace," as implying that gradual giving up of sin. They assume that when persons have stopped sinning, there is no more room for growth in grace. The Bible states that Christ also grew in grace, where the same original word is used as in this command. "He increased in stature, and in wisdom, and in favor (*chariti*—grace) with God and man." If growth in grace implies the gradual giving up of sin, then God has commanded men not to give up their sins at once—they must give them up gradually. The truth is that growth in grace implies the immediate relinquishment of sin to begin with. To grow in grace is to grow in the favor of God. And what would the Apostle have said, had he supposed that the requirement to grow in grace would have been understood by an orthodox Church to require only the gradual relinquishment of their sins? I suppose that saints will continue to grow in grace and in the knowledge

---

*See especially Finney's book *Principles of Union With Christ*, published by Bethany House Publishers, for his thorough, practical application of this point.

of God throughout eternity. But this does not imply that they are not entirely holy when they enter heaven or before they enter heaven.

29. Entire sanctification does not imply that others will recognize it to be real sanctification. *With the present views of the Church in regard to what is implied in entire sanctification, it is impossible that a really sanctified soul should be acknowledged by the Church as such.* With the current view of the Church, there is no doubt that sanctified believers would be discredited, and denounced by the majority of Christians in regards to their claim of having a sanctified spirit.

The Jews believed and positively insisted that Jesus Christ was possessed by a wicked, instead of a holy, spirit. So distorted were their notions of holiness that they no doubt supposed Him to be motivated by something other than the Spirit of God. They were totally convinced of it on account of His opposition to the current orthodoxy and the ungodliness of the religious teachers of the day. Likewise, when the Church finds herself greatly conformed to the world, it follows that the spirit of holiness in any man would certainly lead him to aim his sharpest rebukes at the spirit and life of those in this state of conformity, no matter what their position. And who does not see that this would naturally result in his being accused of possessing a wicked spirit?

The most violent opposition that I have ever seen manifested to any persons in my life has been manifested by members of the Church, and even by some ministers of the gospel, toward those who I believe were among the most holy persons I ever knew. I have been shocked, and wounded beyond expression, at the almost fiendish opposition to such persons that I have witnessed.

At one time, writers in newspapers were asking for examples of Christian perfection or entire sanctification. What use is it to point the Church to examples as long as they do not know what is and what is not implied in a state of entire sanctification? I would ask, Are those in the Church agreed among themselves with regard to what constitutes this state? Are any considerable number of ministers agreed among themselves as to what is implied in a state of entire sanctification? Does not everybody know that the Church and the ministry, to a great extent, know very little about the subject? Why then call for examples? No man can profess to have attained this state without being sure to be discredited as a hypocrite and a self-deceiver.

30. The state of entire sanctification does not imply that the sanctified soul will himself, always and at all times, be sure that his feelings and conduct are perfectly right. Cases may occur in which he may be in doubt in regard to the rule of duty; and be at a loss, without examination, reflection, and prayer to know whether in a particular case he has done and felt exactly right. If he were sure that he understood the exact application of the law of God to that particular case, his consciousness would invariably inform him whether or not he was conformed to that rule. But if a case should arise where he does not have a clear apprehension of the rule, it may require time, thought, prayer, and diligent inquiry to satisfy his mind in regard to the exact moral quality of any particular act or state of feeling.

For example, a man may feel himself moved with strong indignation in view of sin. He may begin to doubt about whether or not the kind or degree of indignation was sinful. It may, therefore, require self-examination and deep heart searching to decide this question. It is certain that not all indignation is sinful. It is also certain that a particular kind and degree of indignation at sin is a duty. Nonetheless, our most holy exercises may open us up to the assaults of Satan. He may rail accusations at us so that for a time it is difficult for us to decide in regard to the real state of our hearts. Thus, a sanctified soul may be "in heaviness through manifold temptations."

31. Nor does entire sanctification imply the same strength of holy affection that Adam may have exercised before he fell and his faculties were weakened by sin. It should never be forgotten that the mind in this state of existence is wholly dependent upon the brain and physical system for its development. In Adam, and in any of his descendants, any violation of the physical laws of the body, resulting in the weakness and imperfections of any organ or system of organs, must necessarily

impair the vigor of the mind, and prevent its developing to its fullest potential. It is, therefore, entirely erroneous to say that mankind are or can be, in this state of existence, perfect in as high a sense as they might have been had sin never entered the world, and had there been no such thing as a violation of the laws of their physical constitution. The law of God requires only the entire consecration of the powers we have. As these powers improve, our obligation increases and will continue to increase throughout all eternity.

It is my opinion that the human constitution is capable of being very nearly, if not entirely, renovated or recovered from the evils of self-gratification by a right understanding of and an adherence to the laws of life and health. I believe that after a few generations the human body would be nearly, if not entirely, restored to its original physical perfection. If this is so, then the time may come when obedience to the law of God will imply as great a strength and constancy of affection as Adam was capable of exercising before the fall. But if, on the other hand, it is true that any injury of the physical constitution can never be wholly repaired—that the evils of self-gratification in respect to its effect upon the body, are, in some measure at least, to descend with men to the end of time, then no such thing is implied in a state of entire sanctification as the same strength and permanency of holy affection in us that Adam might have exercised before the fall.

Some believe that the Son of God requires us to exercise all the strength and perfection of service which we might have rendered had we never sinned. They argue that although man has, by his own or by Adam's act, lost the power or ability to render the same degree of service which he might have rendered had he never sinned, this inability does not abrogate God's right to require this now impossible service. They say that unless this is so, a man could annihilate his ability and his moral obligation would cease. By sinning, they argue that a man might annihilate his obligation to obedience. To this I reply:

If this objection had come from those who deny the natural ability of man to obey the law of God, and who maintain that no ability whatever is implied in obligation, it would not have been so surprising. But coming as it does from those who maintain the natural ability of men to comply with all the requirements of God, and that natural ability is indispensable to obligation, and who hold the attainableness of entire sanctification on the ground of natural ability, this objection is truly surprising. What consistency is there in maintaining the natural ability of sinners to do their whole duty, and the instantaneous attainableness of a state of entire sanctification on the ground of natural ability, and at the same time asserting that although man has lost the power to render that degree of service to God because of sin, yet the law still holds him bound to render all that service nevertheless? Now what is this but both affirming and denying natural ability in the same breath? It is inconsistent with moral obligation to suppose that man is able to render to God as high and perfect a service at the present time, as if he had never sinned—as if he had never neglected to know all that might be known of God—as if he had fully developed his powers by universal and perfect obedience. And if he is under obligation to do so, in spite of this inability, then to maintain the doctrine of natural ability, or that men are naturally able to comply with all the requirements of God, is absurd and a contradiction.

It is certain man is naturally able to do only that which, under the circumstances, is possible. Nothing is possible to him which he cannot accomplish by willing and honestly endeavoring to do it. But who will maintain, that, by willing, a drunkard can so restore his shattered constitution, as in a moment to have all those bodily energies, upon which the mind is naturally dependent, restored to perfect health, so as to render it possible for him to exercise the same degree of mental vigor that he might have exercised had he never been a drunkard? Or who will say that by willing, he can instantaneously possess all that degree of knowledge of God and divine things which he might have had, were it not for his past neglect? Who will say, that by willing, he can instantaneously exercise his holy affections as fresh, and vigorous, and powerful, and constant, as if his powers had been fully developed by universal and perfect obedience ever since he has existed? Certainly no man will affirm this. As you can see, it is quite evident that man is unable to render to God what he might have done if it hadn't been for his past sin.

And now the question arises, Is he under obligation to render the same service in *degree* as if his powers *were* in that state of perfection in which they would have been had he never sinned? I find it strange that those who maintain the natural ability of sinners to perfectly obey God answer this question affirmatively.

It seems they feel themselves called upon to take this ground to escape the necessity of adopting what they understand to be a wholly untenable position. They claim that if a man impairs his ability to comply with the law of God, he does away with moral obligation. It follows then, that should he utterly destroy his ability to obey, his ability to sin would also cease. At this point let me inquire if this is not really the fact. Do not cases often occur in which men destroy, for the time being, their own moral agency by rendering themselves insane? Now is it not universally admitted that a person in a state of mental derangement is as incapable of moral action as a brute? Is a man in a state of insanity a moral agent? I answer, no. Can he sin? No. Was it ever maintained by any moralist that he could? No.

Nor does it matter by what means he became deranged, if his insanity is real. It is true that courts of law hold insane persons, under certain circumstances, accountable for their conduct. When, for example, a man commits a crime while intoxicated, although at the time it is obvious he was deranged, yet they will punish him for the deed as if he had committed it in the sober exercise of his reason. But the principle upon which they proceed in this case is that the act by which he became insane, namely, his becoming drunk, involves the guilt of the crime which was committed during the time of intoxication. It is not that courts of law ever maintain, that, in such cases, the criminal was a moral agent at the time of his insanity. They do, however, hold him responsible for his conduct, or rather punish him for becoming intoxicated. This they consider as the real issue in which his guilt lies, although in form he is condemned for the crime of which it was the cause.

This same principle applies in the case of sinners under the government of God. When by their own act they lessen their capacity to render to God as high and perfect service as they might have done, their sin lies in that act which lessened their ability. This act constitutes the whole guilt of all the default of which it is the cause. Their guilt, however, does not lie at all in their neglect to do what, after this inability has occurred, they are utterly unable to do. When their powers of moral agency are either destroyed or impaired, by Adam's act—by their parent's act—or by their own act, they are not and cannot by any possibility be under any obligation to use powers which they do not possess. And God has no right to require it of them. But he has a right to hold them responsible and punish them throughout all eternity for the act or neglect that impaired or destroyed their ability. And unless they repent and are forgiven for this abuse of their constitution, it is certain that He will punish them forever.

Now this view of the subject is not at all like that which sets aside the claims of the law by introducing through Christ another rule of duty less opposed to the sinful inclinations of man than is the law of God. My soul abhors this view. The law of God is and always must remain the only rule of duty to moral agents in whatever world or under whatever circumstances they may exist.

But the question which we are trying to resolve is, Does the law of God level its claims to the exact measure of the natural ability of every moral agent? Does it come to him *as he is*, and require the perfect use of his faculties as they are, in His service? Or does it require him to possess other faculties, and to possess them in a different state from what they really are? A demand such as this would be to require impossibilities. God might as well command a man to undo all of his sins, instead of repenting of them—to recall past time, to perform those duties to sinners long dead, which might and ought to have been performed while they were living. Could God justly require this? I answer: no, no more than He could require a dead corpse to raise itself from the dead. God never requires man to perform that which is naturally impossible. To affirm that He does is a slander and a libel upon His character. When a sin has been committed, a duty neglected, and the opportunity and possibility of now performing it has ceased, the only requirement in respect to that is that we repent. And He no longer possesses the right to require of us the performance of that which has become naturally impossible, nor does He in any instance claim or attempt to exercise any such authority as this.

32. The state of entire sanctification does not imply the formation of holy habits which will *secure* obedience. Some have said that it was absurd to profess a state of entire sanctification, on the grounds that it implies not only obedience to the law of God, but such a formation and perfection of holy habits as to render it certain that we shall never sin again. They maintain that a man can no more tell when he is entirely sanctified, than he can tell how many holy acts it will take to form holy habits of such strength that will prevent him from ever sinning again. To this I answer:

a. The law of God has nothing to do with requiring such a formation of holy habits. It is satisfied with present obedience. It only demands at the present moment the full devotion of all our faculties to God. It never, in any instance, complains that we have not formed such holy habits as to render it certain that we shall sin no more.

b. If it is true a man is never wholly sanctified until his holy habits are established so as to render it certain that he will never sin again, then Adam was not in a state of entire sanctification previous to the fall, nor were the angels before their fall.

c. If this view is true, there is not a saint nor an angel in heaven, so far as we can know, that can honestly profess entire sanctification. For how do they know whether they have performed enough holy acts to have created such habits of holiness as to render it certain that they will never sin?

d. Entire sanctification does not consist in formation of holy habits nor depend upon this at all. *Both entire and permanent sanctification are based alone on the grace of God in Jesus Christ. Perseverance in holiness is to be ascribed alone to the influence of the indwelling Spirit of Christ, instead of being secured by any habits of holiness which we have or ever will have formed.*

33. Nor does entire sanctification imply exemption from sorrow or mental suffering.

It was not so with Christ. Nor is it inconsistent with our grieving for our past sins. Nor is it inconsistent with our regretting that we do not now have the health and vigor and knowledge and love that we might have had if we had sinned less. We will sorrow for those around us, sorrowing in view of human sinfulness or suffering. These are all consistent with a state of entire sanctification, and indeed are the natural results of it.

34. Entire sanctification is not inconsistent with our living in human society—with mingling in the scenes and engaging in the affairs of this world. Some have supposed that to be holy we must withdraw from the world. Hence the unnatural practices of those who retire to monasteries and convents and, as they say, to dedicate themselves to a life of devotion. I take this state of voluntary exclusion from human society to be inconsistent with biblical holiness and a manifest violation of the law of love to our neighbor.

35. Nor does entire sanctification imply ill-temper and ill-natured manners. Nothing is further from the truth than this. It is said of Xavier, beside whom, perhaps, few holier men have ever lived, that "he was so cheerful as often to be accused of being jolly." Cheerfulness is certainly the result of holy affections. Sanctification no more implies gloominess in this world than it does in heaven.

Before I proceed in my discourse, (having said these things, and having given these rules of interpretation so that you can apply the principles to the many things I have not had time to mention) I wish to make the following remark:

In all the discussions I have seen on this subject, while it seems to be admitted that the law of God is the standard of perfection, yet in defining what constitutes Christian perfection or entire sanctification, men entirely lose sight of this standard and seldom or never raise the distinct inquiry, What does obedience to this law imply, and what does it not imply? Instead of measuring everything by this standard, they seem to lose sight of it. On the one hand, they present things that never were required by the law of God from man in his present state. Thus they lay a stumbling block and a snare for the saints to keep them in perpetual bondage. They assume that this is the way to keep them humble, by placing the standard entirely above their reach. Or, on the other hand, they really abrogate the law, so as to make it no longer binding. Or they do away with what is really implied in it so as to leave nothing in its requirements but a kind of sickly, whimsical, inefficient sentimentalism, or perfectionism, which in its manifestations and results appears to me to be anything else than that which the law of God requires.

3

WHAT IS ENTIRE SANCTIFICATION?

In answering this question, I will refer to and repeat some things that I have said before in my sermons on the law of God.*

1. *Love is the sum of all that is implied in entire sanctification.* But what kind of love is required? Let me consider separately love toward God and love toward man. First, I will describe *the kind of love which must be exercised toward God.*

It is to be love of the *heart*, and not a mere emotion. By the *heart*, I mean the *will*. Emotions, or what are generally termed feelings, are always involuntary states of mind. Our emotions have moral character only insofar as they are indirectly under the control of the will. Feelings are not choices or volitions, and of course do not govern the conduct. Love, in the form of an emotion, may exist in opposition to the will. We may exercise emotions of love contrary to our conscience and judgment, and in opposition to our will. This explains how men and women often exercise emotions of love toward those to whom all the voluntary powers of the mind feel opposed, and with whom they will not associate. So sinners often *desire* to be Christians, and experience strong emotions on the subject of their salvation, while their will is entirely opposed to God. And hypocrites often experience deep emotions of love toward God, sorrow for sin, and many other classes of emotions, while their will remains

---

*These sermons from *The Oberlin Evangelist* are reprinted in Charles G. Finney, *The Promise of the Spirit*, edited by Timothy Smith (Minneapolis: Bethany House Publishers, 1979).

purely selfish and wholly opposed to God. It is true that in most cases the emotions are in line with the will. But they are often opposed to it.

Now, the law of God requires a voluntary state of mind; that is, it lays its claims upon the will. The will controls the conduct. Therefore, God requires the love of the heart or will.

Benevolence is one of the modifications of love that we are to exercise toward God. Benevolence is good willing. Certainly we are bound to exercise this kind of love toward God. That we should exercise good and not ill will to God is a dictate of reason, of conscience, of common sense and of immutable justice. It does not matter whether He needs our good will, or whether our good or ill will can in any way affect Him. The question does not respect His *needs*, but *what He deserves*: He deserves our love and good will.

God's well-being is certainly an infinite good in itself. Consequently, we are bound to desire it, to will it, to rejoice in it. We must will it and rejoice in it, in proportion to its *intrinsic* importance. Since His well-being is certainly a matter of *infinite* importance, we are under infinite obligation to will it with all our hearts.

Another modification of this love is *complacency* or *esteem*. God's character is infinitely good. We are bound to love Him with the love of benevolence, and to exercise the highest degree of respect for His character. To say that God is good and lovely is merely to say that He deserves to be loved. If He deserves to be loved on account of His goodness and love, then He deserves to be loved in proportion to His goodness and loveliness. Therefore, our greatest obligation is to exercise toward Him the highest degree of the love of complacency of which we are capable. These remarks are confirmed by the Bible, by reason, by conscience and by common sense.

Another modification of this love is *gratitude*. Since every moral being is constantly receiving favors from God, it is self-evident that love in the form of gratitude, or the exercise of perfect gratitude, is universally obligatory.

Another peculiarity of this love, which must by no means be overlooked, is that it is *disinterested*. This means that we do not love Him for selfish reasons; we love Him for what He is—with benevolence. Because His well-being is an infinite good, we love Him with complacency. Because His character is infinitely excellent, we love Him with the heart, because all virtue belongs to the heart. Nothing short of disinterested love is virtue. The Savior recognizes and settles this truth: "For if ye love them which love you, what thank have ye? for sinners also love those that love them. And if ye do good to them which do good to you, what thank have ye? for sinners also do even the same. And if you lend to them of whom ye hope to receive, what thank have ye? for sinners also lend to sinners, to receive as much again" (Luke 6:32-34). These words epitomize the whole doctrine of the Bible on this subject, and set forth the plain principle that to love God or any one else for selfish reasons is not virtue.

Another peculiarity of this love is that in every instance it must be *supreme*. Anything less than supreme love to God implies an idolatrous state of mind. If anything else is loved more than God, *that* is our God.

I have been surprised to learn that some understand the term *supreme* in a comparative and not in a superlative sense. They assume that the law of God requires more than supreme love. Webster's definition of supreme and supremely is "in the highest degree," "to the utmost extent." I understand the law to require as high a state of devotion to God, of love and actual service, as the faculties of body and mind are capable of sustaining.

Observe that God lays great stress on the degree of love. The *degree* is essential to the *kind* of love. If it is not *supreme* in *degree*, it is wholly defective and unacceptable to God.

Next, I will consider *the kind of love to be exercised toward our fellow men.*

It must be the love of the *heart*, and not mere desire or emotion. It is very natural to desire the good of others, to pity the distressed, to feel strong emotions of compassion toward those who are afflicted. These emotions, however, are not virtue. Unless we *will* their good, as well as desire it, it is of no avail. "If a brother or sister be naked, and destitute of daily food, and one of you say unto them, Depart in peace, be ye warmed and filled; notwithstanding ye give them not those things which are needful to the body; what doth it profit?" (James 2:15, 16).

The Apostle fully recognizes the principle that mere desire for the good of others, which of course will satisfy itself with good words instead of good works, is not virtue. Good *willing*, instead of just good *desiring*, will produce corresponding action. Without good willing, there is no true holiness.

Benevolence to men is a prime manifestation of holy love. Though this is included in what I have mentioned above, it needs to be expressly stated and explained. It is a plain dictate of reason, of conscience, of common sense and immutable justice that we should exercise good will toward our fellow men. We should will their good in proportion to its relative importance. We should rejoice in their happiness and endeavor to promote it according to their relative value in the scale of being.

Complacency (respect) toward those who are virtuous is another modification of holy love to men. I say toward those that are *virtuous*, because while we exercise *benevolence toward all*, irrespective of their character, we have a right to exercise *complacency* only toward those who are holy. To exercise complacency toward the wicked is to be as wicked as they are. But to exercise entire complacency in those who are holy is to be holy ourselves.

Holy love is to be equal in every instance. By equal, I do not mean that degree of love which selfish beings have for themselves, for this is supreme selfishness. There is a great distinction between self-love and selfishness. *Self-love is that desire of happiness and dread of misery which is inherent to our nature. Selfishness is the excess of self-love; it is making our own happiness the supreme object of pursuit, because it is our own.* In not placing importance on the other's interests and happiness, which their relative value demands, a selfish mind is, therefore, exercising the supreme love of self.

Now the law of God does not require or permit us to love our neighbor with the supreme degree of love, for that would be idolatry. But the command, "to love our neighbor as ourselves," implies, that we should love ourselves less than supremely, and attach no more importance to our own interests and happiness than their relative value demands. We also must love our neighbor with the same degree of love which is *lawful* for us to exercise toward ourselves.

Equal love does not imply that we should neglect our own *appropriate* concerns and attend to the affairs of others. God has appointed to every man a particular sphere in which to act and particular affairs to which he must attend. And this business, whatever it is, must be transacted for God and not for ourselves. For a man to neglect his particular calling, under the pretense of attending to the business of others, is neither required nor permitted by this law.

We are not to neglect our own families and the nurture and education of our children to attend to that of others. "But if any provide not for his own, and specially for those of his own house, he hath denied the faith, and is worse than an infidel" (1 Tim. 5:8). We are to attend to these duties for God. No man or woman is required or permitted to neglect the children God has given them under the pretense of attending to the families of others.

The law does not require or permit us to squander our possessions on those who are drunken, immoral and lazy. Not that we should never relieve the absolute necessities of such persons, but we must always do it in such a manner as not to encourage, but rather rebuke their evil lifestyles. Nor does this law require or permit us to let others live by sponging off our possessions, while they themselves are not engaged in promoting the good of men. It does not require or permit us to lend money to speculators, or for speculating purposes, or in any way to encourage selfishness.

By *equal* love, I mean the same love in *kind* and *degree*, which it is lawful for us to exercise toward ourselves. It is not only lawful, but *it is our duty to exercise an appropriate concern for our own happiness, the same degree we are required to exercise for the happiness of all our fellow men.*

Another feature of holy love is that it is *impartial*; that is, it extends to *enemies* as well as *friends*. Otherwise, it is selfish love and comes under the reprobation of the Savior in the passage quoted above: "For if ye love them which love you, what thank have ye? for sinners also love those that love them" (Luke 6:32–34).

This test must always be applied to the *kind* of love we exercise toward our fellow men, in order to understand its *genuineness*. God's love is love to enemies. He gave His Son for His enemies. Our love must be the same kind—it must extend to enemies as well as to friends. And if it does not, it is partial and selfish.

2. *Entire sanctification implies entire conformity of the heart and life to all the known will of God, however it may be made known, to both physical and moral law so far as they are known.*

3. Entire sanctification implies such a perfect confidence in Him that we are willing to entrust all events to His sovereign control. This confidence must preclude all worry and undue anxiety about ourselves or our friends, our temporal or eternal interests, the interests of the Church or of the world. Do not misunderstand me. I do not mean that a state of entire sanctification is inconsistent with the greatest desire and most earnest and prevailing wrestlings with God for blessings both spiritual and temporal for ourselves and the world. I do, however, mean that a soul that is entirely conformed to the will of God will never so distrust His providence and grace as to be thrown into a state of frantic anxiety about any event. Such a soul will, on all occasions, in child-like faith, consent and rejoice in the will of God in whatever way that will is revealed.

4. Entire sanctification implies a supreme disposition to glorify and serve God. The ruling principle of our life is to glorify God. We no longer live for any other end. All the things we desire we view as a means to this end: life and health, food and clothing, houses and furniture, and everything else we possess we regard as a means to this one great absorbing end, the Glory of God.

5. Entire sanctification implies such a degree of energy in the principle of love that it directly or indirectly controls every design and every voluntary action.

6. Entire sanctification implies an abiding sense of the presence of God. From what I have already said, you will understand that I do not mean that God is to be at all times the direct

object of thought, attention and affection. Nonetheless, there should be such a sense of His presence at all times that this has an important and efficient influence on our whole lives. Everyone knows by his own experience what it is like to have a kind of sense or consciousness or felt conviction of the presence of a person, who at the time is not the direct object of our thoughts. A man in the presence of an earthly prince, or a grand court, or under the eye of a human judge, would be continually awed and restrained and affected with a kind of sense of where he was, and in whose presence, and under whose eye he was acting, although his mind might be so intensely employed in the transaction of business at hand as not to make the judge or prince the object of his direct thought, attention or affection at all. In this sense, a sanctified soul will have an abiding sense of the presence of God at all times and in all places. When the mind is withdrawn from necessary pursuits, it will naturally return to God and be aware of His presence in a vastly higher sense than this. It will be so impressed and overwhelmed by a sense of His presence that could never be expressed in words, but as a matter of experience is familiar to all those who walk with God.

7. Entire sanctification implies deep and uninterrupted communion with God. But here let me correct a mistake into which, I believe, some have fallen. Many seem to only recognize communion with God as that sweet peace and joy, that continual glowing love that the soul often experiences in seasons of communion. But God, no doubt, often has times of communication and communion with the sanctified soul when He reminds it of past sins and follies. And in order to keep it in a sanctified state, He gives it such a view of its past history as to fill it with unutterable shame, self-abhorrence and self-contempt. People are apt to view this state of mind as one of darkness, and to think that God is hiding His countenance from them, when, in fact, they are perhaps never more thoroughly in the light than at such times. The truth is, that on such occasions, they may be nearer than ever to God. Obviously, their thoughts are not occupied with those sweet and heavenly visions that fill the mind with joy. Yet they are occupied with

considerations of no less importance, and no less indispensable to continuing them in a state of holiness than those sweet truths which at other times so greatly rejoice them.

8. Entire sanctification implies a greater dread of offending God than of any other evil. This is implied in supreme love. To say that we love God supremely and yet do not dread offending Him as much as we dread some other evil is a contradiction. If we love Him more than any earthly friend, we will dread offending Him more than offending that friend. If we love Him more than we do ourselves, we will dread offending Him more than some evil should happen to us. If He is dearer to us than our own souls, we will dread remaining in sin more than we dread the loss of our souls.

9. Entire sanctification implies the subjection of all our appetites and passions to the will of God. *I have already said that the sin of Adam consisted in preferring the gratification of his appetites rather than doing the will of God. This is the sin of all men. This is the substance and the history of selfishness.* Entire obedience to the law of God implies that no appetite or feeling of body or mind will be gratified in opposition to the known will of God. "The whole body, soul, and spirit" will be sustained in a state of entire consecration to God.

10. Entire sanctification implies diligent stewardship of our time in the acquisition of knowledge and a consecration of what we already know to the service of God.

I have said before that the legal maxim, "Ignorance of the law excuses no one," is true in morals only to a limited extent, and that under the government of God, actual knowledge is indispensable to obligation. I think this was adequately proved by a reference to scriptural testimony. I also said that in sins of ignorance, the sin lies in the ignorance itself, and not in the neglect of performing that of which the mind has no knowledge.

Now to avoid mistake, it is important to emphasize here that *ignorance of our duty is always a sin when we possess the means and opportunity of information. In such cases, the guilt of the ignorance is equal to all the default that it causes.* Strictly speaking, the duty to do a thing does not become moral obligation until the mind has a knowledge of that thing. Yet if the means of knowledge are attainable, the guilt is just as great as all the default which this ignorance caused. In the case of civil government, courts of law do not perform injustice by holding all the citizens of that government responsible for not knowing the law, *where the means* of attaining that knowledge are within their reach. Although, in form, they are not pronounced guilty for their ignorance, and punished for that specific offense, on the contrary, they are held responsible for breaches of those laws of which they had no knowledge; yet, in fact, no injustice is done them, as their ignorance in such cases really deserves the punishment inflicted.

Some may object to this, saying that God, under the old dispensation, treated sins of ignorance as involving less guilt than sins committed against knowledge. To this I reply:

That is indeed the case, and the reason is very obvious. The people possessed very limited means of information. Copies of the law were very scarce and utterly inaccessible to the great mass of the people. So that while He held them sufficiently responsible to engage their memories to retain a knowledge of their duty, and to search it out with all diligence, yet it is plain that He held them responsible in a vastly lower sense than He does those who have higher means of information. The responsibility of the heathen was less than that of the Jews—that of the Jews less than that of Christians—and that of Christians in the early ages of the Church, before the canon of Scripture was complete and copies multiplied, much less than that of Christians of the present day.

11. Entire sanctification implies the complete annihilation of selfishness in all its forms, and a practical and heartfelt recognition of the rights and interests of our neighbor. Let me point out a few specifics of what the law of God prohibits and what it requires in these particulars.

a. It prohibits all *supreme self-love* or selfishness. The command, "Love thy neighbor as thy self," implies, not that we should love our neighbor supremely, as selfish men love themselves; but that we should love ourselves, in the first place, and pursue our happiness, only according to our relative value in the scale of being. I need not dwell on this, for it is self-evident this precept prohibits *supreme* self-love.

b. It prohibits all *excessive* self-love; that is, every degree of love that is disproportioned to the relative value of our own happiness.

c. It prohibits laying any practical stress on any interest simply because it is our *own*.

d. It prohibits, of course, every degree of *ill-will*, and all those feelings that are necessarily connected with selfishness.

e. It prohibits *apathy* and *indifference* in regard to the well-being of our fellow men.

f. It does require the practical recognition of the fact that all men are brethren—that God is the great Father of the universe—that all moral agents everywhere are His children—and that He is interested in the happiness of every individual according to its relative importance. He is no respector of persons. He loves all moral beings in proportion to their capacity of receiving and doing good.

The law of God evidently takes all of this for granted, that God "hath made of one blood all nations of men for to dwell on all the face of the earth" (Acts 17:26).

g. It requires that every being and interest should be regarded and treated by us *according to its relative value*; that is, that we should recognize God's relation to the universe, and our relation to each other, and treat all men as our brethren. All men have a God-given right to our good will as citizens of the same government, and members of His great family.

h. It requires us to exercise the same tender regard to our neighbor's *reputation, interest, and well-being,* in all respects, as to our own. We must be as unwilling to mention his faults, as to have our own mentioned—to hear him slandered as to be slandered ourselves. In short, we are to esteem him as our brother.

i. It justly condemns any violation of the great principle of equal love as *rebellion* against the whole universe. It is rebellion against God because it is a rejection of His authority. Selfishness, in any form, is a setting up of our own interests in opposition to the interests of the universe of God.

12. Entire sanctification implies a willingness to exercise

self-denial, even unto death, for the glory of God and good of man if necessary. The Apostle teaches us that "we ought to lay down our lives for the brethren" (1 John 3:16), as Christ laid down His.

We have now arrived at a very important point in the discussion of this subject. Having discussed,

1. What I mean by the term sanctification;

2. What entire sanctification is;

3. The distinction between entire and permanent sanctification;

4. What is not implied in entire sanctification, and

5. What is implied in entire sanctification;

I will next, according to my plan, show that entire and permanent sanctification is attainable in this life.

4

INTERPRETING GOD'S PROMISES

In this chapter and the following two, I will explain in several different ways *that entire and permanent sanctification is attainable in this life.*

1. Entire obedience to God's law is possible on the ground of natural ability. This is self-evident. To deny this is to deny that a man is able to do as well as he can. The very language of the law levels its claims to the capacity of the subject, however great or small that capacity may be. "Thou shalt love the Lord thy God with all thy heart, and with all thy soul, and with all thy mind, and with all thy strength." All the law demands is that we exercise whatever strength we have in the service of God. Now, since entire sanctification consists of perfect obedience to the law of God, and since the law requires nothing more than the right use of whatever strength we have, it is, of course, forever settled that a state of entire and permanent sanctification is attainable in this life on the ground of natural ability.

New School theologians generally admit this. Or perhaps I should say, it has been generally admitted by them, though at present some of them seem inclined to give up the doctrine of natural ability and take refuge in physical depravity, rather than admit the attainableness of a state of entire sanctification in this life. But let men take refuge where they will, they can never escape from the plain letter and spirit and meaning of the law of God. The Bible clearly states, "Thou shalt love the Lord thy God with all thy heart, and with all thy soul, and with

55

all thy mind, and with all thy strength." This is the law's solemn injunction, whether it be given to an angel, a man or a child. An angel is bound to exercise an angel's strength; a man, the strength of a man; and a child, the strength of a child. This law comes to every moral being in the universe just as he is, and where he is. The law does not require him to create new powers or possess other powers than he has. It does, however, require him to use the powers he has with the utmost perfection and constancy for God.

To use the language of a respected brother, "If we could conceive of a moral pigmy, the law levels its claims to his capacities, and says to him, 'Love the Lord thy God with all thy heart, and with all thy strength.'" And should a man by his own fault render himself unable to use one of his hands, feet, or any power of body or mind, the law does not demand him in that case to use all the powers and strength he might have had, but only what powers and strength remain. It holds him guilty and condemns him for that act or neglect which diminished his ability, and pronounces a sentence upon him commensurate with all the guilt of all the default of which that act was the cause. But it no longer, in any instance, requires the use of that power of body or mind which has been destroyed by that act.

2. The provisions of grace are more than sufficient to make the actual attainment of entire sanctification in this life an object of reasonable pursuit. The entire and permanent sanctification of the Church is to be accomplished. It is admitted that this work is to be accomplished "through the sanctification of the Spirit and the belief of the truth." It is also universally agreed that this work must be begun here, and that it must be completed before the soul can enter heaven. The logical question to ask is:

Is this state attainable as a matter of fact before death? If so, when in this life may we expect to attain it?

This question can only be settled by referring to the Word of God. And it is extremely important that we understand the rules by which we are to interpret Scripture declarations and promises. I have already given several rules which we have endeavored to use to interpret the meaning of the law. I will now state several plain common-sense rules by which we are to interpret the *promises*. The question regarding the rules of biblical interpretation is fundamental to all religious inquiry. Until the whole Church agrees to interpret the Scriptures in accordance with certain fixed and undeniable principles, they can never be agreed with regard to what the Bible teaches. I have often been amazed at the total disregard of all sound rules of biblical interpretation. The warnings or the promises are either thrown away or made to mean something entirely different from what was intended by the Spirit of God.

I will proceed to mention only a few plain, common-sense and self-evident rules for the interpretation of the promises. In the light of these, we may be able to settle the following question: Are the provisions of grace more than sufficient to make the actual attainment of entire and permanent sanctification in this life an object of reasonable pursuit?

(1) The language of a promise is to be interpreted with reference to the known character of the one who promises, where this character is revealed and made known in other ways than by the promise itself. For example, if the promisor is known to be of a very willing disposition, or the opposite of this, these considerations should be taken into account when interpreting the language of his promise. If he is of a very bountiful disposition, he may be expected to mean all that he seems to mean in the language of his promise, and a *very* liberal construction should be put upon his language. But if his character is known to be the opposite of bountifulness, and if it is known that whatever he promised would be given with great reluctance, his language should be construed strictly.

An inclination to use hyperbole and extravagance should be taken into account when interpreting his promises. If the promisor is in the habit of using extravagant language; if he says much more than he means, this should be taken into account when interpreting his promises. But on the other hand, if he is known to be a very honest individual who uses language with great care and relevance, then we may freely understand him to mean what he says. His promise may be in figurative language—not to be understood literally—but even in his case, we must understand him to mean what the figure naturally and fully implies.

The fact should be taken into account whether or not the promise was made deliberately or under circumstances of great but temporary excitement. If the promise was made deliberately, it should be interpreted to mean what it says. But if it was made under great but temporary excitement, we need to make allowance for the state of mind which led to the use of such strong language.

(2) The relation of the parties to each other should be properly considered in the interpretation of the language of a promise. For example, the promise of a father to a son suggests a more liberal and bountiful construction than if the promise were made to a stranger. A father may be supposed to cherish a more liberal and bountiful disposition toward a son than toward a person in whom he has no particular interest.

(3) The intention of the promisor in relation to the needs of the promisee, or person to whom the promise is made, should be taken into the account. If it is clear the intention of the promisor was to meet the needs of the promisee, then his promise must be so understood as to meet these needs.

(4) If it is clear the intention of the promisor was to meet the needs of the promisee, then the extent of these needs should be taken into account in the interpretation of the promise.

(5) The interest of the promisor in accomplishing his intentions or in fully meeting and relieving the needs of the promisee should be taken into account. If there is satisfactory proof, other than the promise itself, that the promisor feels the highest interest in the promisee and in fully meeting and relieving his needs, then his promise must be understood accordingly.

(6) If it is known that the promisor has exercised the greatest self-denial and made the greatest sacrifice for the promisee in order to make it proper or possible for him to make and fulfill his promises in relation to meeting his needs, the state of mind implied in this conduct should be fully recognized in interpreting the language of the promise. It would be utterly unreasonable and absurd, in this case, to restrict the language of his promise and make it fall entirely short of what might reason-

ably be expected of the promisor from those developments of his character, feelings and intentions which were made by the great self-denial he has exercised and the sacrifice he has made.

(7) The effect of the promise on the interests of the promisor should also be taken into account. A general and correct rule of interpretation states that when the thing promised has detrimental effect on the interest of the promisor, and is something which he cannot well afford to do and might therefore be supposed to promise with reluctance, the language in such a case is to be strictly interpreted. No more is to be understood by it than the strictest interpretation will demand.

(8) If on the other hand, the thing promised will not impoverish or be antagonistic in any way to the interests of the promisor, no such interpretation is to be resorted to.

(9) Where the thing promised is that which the promisor has the greatest delight in doing or bestowing; where he accounts it "more blessed to give than to receive"; where it is well known by other revelations of his character, and by his own direct and often repeated declarations, that he has the highest satisfaction and finds his own happiness in bestowing favors upon the promisee, in this case the most liberal interpretation should be put upon the promise. He is to be understood to mean all that he says.

(10) The resources and ability of the promisor to meet the necessities of the promisee without injury to himself are to be considered. If a physician should promise to restore a patient to *perfect* health, it might be unfair to understand him as meaning all that he says. If he treated the patient so that he recovered almost totally from his disease, it might be reasonable to suppose that this was all he really intended. The known inability of a physician to restore an individual to *perfect* health might reasonably modify our understanding of the language of his promise. But when there can be no doubt as to the ability, resources and willingness of the physician to restore his patient to *perfect* health, then we are, in all reason and justice, required to believe he means all that he says. If God should promise to restore a man to *perfect* health who was diseased, there can be no doubt that His promise should be understood to mean what its language conveys.

(11) When *commands* and *promises* are given by one person to another in the same language, in both cases it is to be understood alike, unless there is some obvious reason to the contrary.

(12) If neither the language, context, nor circumstances demand a different interpretation, we are bound to understand the same language alike in both cases.

(13) I have mentioned before that we are to interpret the language of the law so as to agree with natural justice. I now say that we are to interpret the language of the promises so as to agree with the known greatness, resources, goodness, bountifulness, relations, design, happiness and glory of the promisor.

(14) If his bountifulness is equal to his justice, his promises of grace must be understood to mean as much as the requirements of his justice.

(15) If he delights in giving as much as in receiving, his promises must mean as much as the language of his requirements.

(16) If he is as merciful as he is just, his promises of mercy must be as liberally interpreted as the requirements of his justice.

(17) If "he delighteth in mercy," and says, "judgment is his strange work," and mercy is that in which he has peculiar satisfaction, his promises of grace and mercy are to be understood even more liberally than the commands and warnings of his justice. The language in this case is to be understood as meaning quite as much as the same language would in any supposable circumstances.

(18) Another rule of interpreting and applying the promises, which has been extensively overlooked, is this: the promises are all "yea and amen in Christ Jesus." They are all founded on and expressive of the great and immutable principles of God's government. God is no respector of persons. He knows nothing of favoritism. But when He makes a promise, He reveals a principle of universal application to all persons in similar circumstances. Therefore, the promises are not restricted in their application to the individual or individuals to whom they were first given, but may be claimed by anyone in similar circum-

stances. What God is at one time, He always is. What He has promised at one time or to one person, *He promises at all times to anyone under similar circumstances.* It is evident that this is a correct view of the subject from the manner in which the New Testament writers understood and applied the promises of the Old Testament.

Let any person, with a reference Bible, read the New Testament with a purpose to understand how its writers applied the promises of the Old Testament, and he will see this principle brought out in all its fullness. It is true regarding all the promises made to Adam, Noah, Abraham, the Patriarchs, and to the inspired men of every age, together with the promises made to the Church, and indeed all the promises of spiritual blessings— what God has said and promised once, He always says and promises to all persons at all times and in all places where similar circumstances exist.

Having stated the rules by which we are to interpret the language of the promises, let us consider the necessary conditions for the fulfillment of a promise.

All the promises of sanctification in the Bible, by their very nature, necessarily imply our active involvement in receiving the thing promised. Since sanctification consists in the right exercise of our own agency, or in obedience to the law of God, a promise of sanctification must necessarily be conditioned on the exercise of faith in the promise. And its fulfillment implies the exercise of our own powers in receiving it.

Consequently, it follows that a promise of sanctification, to be of any avail to us, must be due at a certain time, expressed or implied in the promise. That is, the time must be so fixed, either expressly or impliedly, as to place us in an attitude of waiting for its fulfillment, with daily or hourly expectation of receiving the blessing. If the fulfillment of the promise implies the exercise of our own agency, the promise means nothing to us, unless we are able to understand at what time we are to expect and request its fulfillment.

The promise of Christ to the Apostles concerning the outpouring of the Spirit on the day of Pentecost may illustrate my meaning. He had promised that they would receive the baptism of the Holy Spirit not many days hence. This indication of time was definite enough to place them in an attitude of continual waiting on the Lord with a constant expectation of receiving His promise. Since the baptism of the Holy Spirit involved the exercise of their own agency, it is easy to see that this expectation was indispensable to their receiving the blessing. But, had they understood Christ to promise this blessing at a time vaguely in the future, so as to leave them without the daily expectation of receiving it, they might have, and doubtless would have, gone about their business until He gave further indication that He was about to bestow it. This would place them in an attitude of waiting for its fulfillment.

A promise in the present tense is on demand. In other words, it is always due and its fulfillment may be requested and claimed by the promisee at any time.

A promise due at a future specified time is on demand after that time, and may at any time thereafter be plead as a promise in the present tense.

A great many of the Old Testament promises became due at the coming of Christ. Since that time they are to be considered and used as promises in the present tense. The Old Testament saints could not request their fulfillment because they were either expressly or impliedly informed that they were not to be fulfilled until the coming of Christ. All those promises, therefore, that became due "in the last days," "at the end of the world," that is, the Jewish dispensation, are to be regarded as now due or as promises in the present tense.

Even though these promises are now due, they are expressly or impliedly conditioned on the exercise of faith and our right use of the appropriate means to receive their fulfillment.

When a promise is due, we may expect the fulfillment of it at once or gradually, according to the nature of the blessing. The promise that the world will be converted in the latter days does not imply that we are to expect the world to be converted at any one moment of time. But, the Lord will commence it at once and hasten it in its time, according to the faith and efforts of the Church. On the other hand, when the thing promised may in its nature be fulfilled at once, and when the nature of the case makes it necessary that it should be, then its fulfill-ment may be expected whenever we exercise faith.

There is a plain distinction between promises of grace and of glory. Promises of glory are, of course, not to be fulfilled until we are in heaven. Promises of grace, unless there be some express or implied reason to the contrary, are to be understood as applicable to this life.

A promise may be conditioned in one sense and uncondi-tioned in another. For example, promises made to the Church as a body may be absolute, and their fulfillment secure and certain sooner or later. However, their fulfillment to any gen-eration of the Church, or to any particular individuals of the Church, may be and must be conditioned on their faith and the appropriate use of means. Thus, the promise of God that the Church should possess the land of Canaan was absolute and unconditioned in the sense that the Church, at some period, would, and certainly must take possession of that land. But the promise was conditional in the sense that entering into their possession, by any generation, depended entirely upon their own faith and appropriate use of means. So the promise of the world's conversion, and the sanctification of the Church under the reign of Christ, is unconditional in the sense that it is cer-tain that those events will at some time occur. But *when* they will occur, and *what* generation of individuals will receive this blessing, is necessarily conditioned on their faith. This princi-ple is plainly recognized by the writer of Hebrews: "Seeing therefore it remaineth that some must enter therein, and they to whom it was first preached entered not in because of unbelief . . . Let us labour therefore to enter into that rest, lest any man fall after the same example of unbelief" (Heb. 4:6, 11).

5

PROMISES OF ENTIRE SANCTIFICATION

Using the principles of biblical interpretation presented in the previous chapter, I will now honestly examine the question of *whether entire and permanent sanctification is, in such a sense, attainable in this life so as to make its attainment an object of our rational pursuit.*

Let me first, however, remind you of what this blessing is. *Simple obedience to the law of God is what I understand to be present sanctification, and its continuance to be permanent sanctification.* The law is and forever must be the only standard. Whatever departs from this law on either side must be false. Whatever requires more or less than the law of God I reject as having nothing to do with the question.

I do not intend to examine a great number of Scripture promises, but rather to show that those which I do examine fully sustain the position I have taken. One promise is sufficient to settle this question forever, if it is full and its application just. My purpose now is to examine only a few promises more critically than I did before. This will enable you to apply the same principles to your examination of the Scripture promises generally.

1. Let us begin by referring to the law of God, as given in Deuteronomy 10:12: "And now, Israel, what doth the Lord thy God require of thee, but to fear the Lord thy God, to walk in all his ways, and to love Him, and to serve the Lord thy God with

all thy heart and with all thy soul." I make the following observations on this passage:

a. It clearly sums up the whole duty of man to God—to fear and love Him with all the heart and all the soul.

b. Although this verse is directed to Israel, it is also true of all men. It is equally binding on everyone, and is all that God requires of any man in regard to Him.

c. Obedience to this requirement is entire sanctification.

See Deuteronomy 30:6: "And the Lord thy God will circumcise thine heart, and the heart of thy seed, to love the Lord thy God with all thine heart, and with all thy soul, that thou mayest live." Here we have a promise expressed in the same language as the command just quoted. I make the following observations on this passage:

a. It promises just what the law requires. It promises all that the first and great commandment in any way requires.

b. Obedience to the first commandment always implies obedience to the second. It is plainly impossible that we should "love God, whom we have not seen," and "not love our neighbor whom we have seen."

c. This promise, at face value, appears to mean just what the law means—to promise just what the law requires.

d. If the law requires a state of entire sanctification, then this is a promise of entire sanctification.

e. Since the command is universally binding on all and applicable to all, this promise is likewise universally applicable to all who will lay hold of it.

f. Faith is an indispensable condition for the fulfillment of this promise of sanctification. It is entirely impossible that we should love God with all the heart without confidence in Him. God inspires love in man in no other way than by revealing himself in such a way as to inspire confidence—that confidence which works by love. In Rules Ten and Eleven, for the interpretation of the promises, I stated that "where a command and a promise are given in the same language, we are obligated to interpret the language alike in both cases, unless there is some obvious reason for a different interpretation." Now here there is a perceivable reason why we should understand the language of the promise as meaning as much as the language of the command. This promise appears to have been designed to cover the whole ground of the requirement.

g. Suppose the language in this promise were used in a command, or the form of it were changed into that of a command. Suppose God should say as He does elsewhere, "Thou shalt love the Lord thy God with all thy heart and with all thy soul"; who would doubt that God designed to require a state of entire sanctification or consecration to himself? How then are we to understand it when used in the form of a promise? See Rules Fourteen and Fifteen: "If his bountifulness equals his justice, his promises of grace must be understood to mean as much as the requirements of his justice." "If he delights in giving as much as in receiving, his promises must mean as much as the language of his requirements."

h. This promise of entire sanctification is designed to be fulfilled in this life. The language and context imply this: "I will circumcise thy heart, and the heart of thy seed, to love the Lord thy God with all thy heart, and with all thy soul."

i. Regarding the Church, at some day this promise must be absolute and certain. At some period, God will undoubtedly bring about this state of mind in the Church. But to what particular individuals and generation this promise will be fulfilled must depend upon their faith in the promise.

2. Next look at Jeremiah 31:31-34: "Behold, the days come, saith the Lord, that I will make a new covenant with the house of Israel, and with the house of Judah: not according to the covenant that I made with their fathers in the day that I took them by the hand to bring them out of the land of Egypt; which my covenant they brake, although I was an husband unto them, saith the Lord: but this shall be the covenant that I will make with the house of Israel; After those days, saith the Lord, I will put my law in their inward parts, and write it in their hearts; and will be their God, and they shall be my people. And they shall teach no more every man his neighbor, and every man his brother, saying, Know the Lord: for they shall all know me, from the least of them unto the greatest of them, saith the Lord: for I will forgive their iniquity, and I will remember their sin

no more." I make the following observations on this passage:

a. The promise was to come due, or the time of its fulfillment might be claimed and expected, at the coming of Christ. This is unequivocally settled in Hebrews 8:8-12, where this passage is quoted as being applicable to the gospel day.

b. This promise undeniably refers to entire sanctification. It is a promise that the "law shall be written in the heart." It means that the very temper and spirit required by the law will be forged in the soul. Now, if the law requires entire sanctification or perfect holiness, this is certainly a promise of it; for it is a promise of all that the law requires. To say that this is not a promise of entire sanctification is the same absurdity as to say that perfect obedience to the law is not entire sanctification; and this last is the same absurdity as to say that something more is our duty than what the law requires; and this again is to say that the law is imperfect and unjust.

c. A permanent state of sanctification is plainly implied in this promise. The reason for setting aside the first covenant was because it was broken: "Which my covenant they brake." One great purpose of the New Covenant is that it shall not be broken, for then it would be no better than the first.

Permanency is implied in the fact that it is to be engraven in the heart. It is also plainly implied in the assertion that God will remember their sin no more. In Jeremiah 32:39, 40, where essentially the same promise is repeated, it is clearly stated that the covenant is to be "everlasting"; and that He will so, "put [his] fear in their hearts, that they shall not depart from [him]." Here, the promise of permanency is expressly promised.

Suppose the language of this promise were used in the form of a command. Suppose God were to say, "Let my law be within your hearts, and let it be in your inward parts; and let my fear be so within your hearts that you shall not depart from me. Let your covenant with me be everlasting." If this language were found in a command, would any man in his senses doubt that it meant perfect and permanent sanctification? If not, by what rule of sound interpretation does he make it mean anything else when found in a promise? When such language is found in a promise, to make it mean less than it does when found in a command appears to be profane trifling with the Word of God. See Rule Seventeen, interpretation of the promises.

d. Regarding the Church, this promise, at some period of its history, is unconditional and its fulfillment certain. But in regard to any particular individuals or generations of the Church, its fulfillment is necessarily conditioned upon their faith.

e. The Church, as a body, has certainly never received this New Covenant. Yet doubtless multitudes in every age of the Christian dispensation have received it. And God will hasten the time when it will be so fully accomplished that no one will need say to his brother, "Know the Lord, for all shall know [him], from the least to the greatest."

f. Notice carefully that this promise was made to the Christian Church and not at all to the Jews under the old dispensation. The saints under the old dispensation had no reason to expect the fulfillment of this and similar promises to themselves, because their fulfillment was expressly deferred until the commencement of the Christian dispensation.

g. It has been said that nothing more than regeneration is promised. But were not the Old Testament saints regenerated? Yet, it is expressly said that they did not receive the promises. See Hebrews 11:13, 39, 40: "These all died in faith, not having received the promises, but having seen them afar off, and were persuaded of them, and embraced them, and confessed that they were strangers and pilgrims on the earth . . . And these all, having obtained a good report through faith, received not the promise: God having provided some better thing for us, that they without us should not be made perfect." Here we see that the Old Testament saints did not receive these promises. Yet they were regenerated.

h. It has been said that the promise implies no more than the final perseverance of the saints. But I would question, Did not the Old Testament saints persevere? And yet we have just seen that the Old Testament saints did not receive these promises in their fulfillment.

3. I will next examine the promise in Ezekiel 36:25-27: "Then will I sprinkle clean water upon you, and ye shall be clean:

from all your filthiness, and from all your idols, will I cleanse you. A new heart also will I give you, and a new spirit will I put within you: and I will take away the stony heart out of your flesh, and I will give you an heart of flesh. And I will put my spirit within you, and cause you to walk in my statutes, and ye shall keep my judgments, and do them." I make the following observations on this passage:

a. It was written within nineteen years after those verses we have just examined in Jeremiah. It plainly refers to the same time and is a promise of the same blessing.

b. It seems quite clear, without denial, that this is a promise of entire sanctification. The language is very definite and all-inclusive. "Then," referring to some future time when it should become due, "will I sprinkle clean water upon you, and ye shall be clean." Notice, the first promise is, "ye shall be clean." If to be "clean" does not mean entire sanctification, what does it mean?

The second promise is, "from all your filthiness, and from all your idols, will I cleanse you." If to be cleansed "from all filthiness and all idols," is not a state of entire sanctification, what is?

The third promise is, "a new heart also will I give you, and a new spirit will I put within you: and I will take away the stony heart out of your flesh, and I will give you an heart of flesh." If to have a "clean heart," a "new heart," a "heart of flesh," in opposition to a "heart of stone," is not entire sanctification, what is?

The fourth promise is, "I will put my spirit within you, and cause you to walk in my statutes, and ye shall keep my judgments, and do them."

c. Let us turn the language of these promises into that of command, and understand God as saying, "Make yourself a clean heart, a new heart, and a new spirit; put away all your iniquities, all your filthiness, and all your idols; walk in my statutes, and keep my judgments, and do them." Now what man in the sober exercise of his reason would doubt whether God meant to require a state of entire sanctification in such commands as these? The rules of legal interpretation would demand that we should understand Him accordingly. Rule Five: "The interest of the promisor in accomplishing his intentions or in fully meeting and relieving the necessities of the promisee should also be taken into account. If there is satisfactory proof, other than the promise itself, that the promisor feels the highest interest in the promisee and in fully meeting and relieving his necessities, then his promise must be understood accordingly."

If this is so, what is the fair and proper interpretation of this language when found in a promise? When God uses the same language in a promise as He does in a command, then I see absolutely no doubt as to what He intends to convey by such a promise. For example, see Ezekiel 18:30, 31: "Repent, and turn yourselves from all your transgressions; so iniquity shall not be your ruin. Cast away from you all your transgressions, whereby ye have transgressed; and make you a new heart and a new spirit: for why will you die, O house of Israel?" It is demanded by every sound rule of interpretation that the language in the promise under consideration should mean as much as the language of this command. And who ever dreamed that when he required His people to put away all their iniquities, He only meant that they should put away a part of them?

d. This promise relates to the Church, and it cannot be pretended that it has ever been fulfilled according to its proper meaning in any past age of the Church.

e. As it regards the Church, at a future period of its history this promise is absolute in the sense that it certainly will be fulfilled.

f. It was clearly intended to apply to Christians under the new dispensation, rather than to the Jews under the old dispensation. The sprinkling of clean water and the outpouring of the Spirit seem to plainly indicate the promise belonged more specifically to the Christian dispensation. It undeniably belongs to the same class of promises as those in Jeremiah 31:31-34, Joel 2:28, and many others that clearly look forward to the gospel day as the time when they shall become due. Since these promises have never been fulfilled, in their scope and meaning, their complete fulfillment remains to be realized by the Church as a body. And those individuals and that generation will take possession of the blessing who understand and believe and appropriate them to their own case.

4. Next, I will examine the promise which I quoted at the very beginning, 1 Thessalonians 5:23, 24: "And the very God of peace sanctify you wholly; and I pray God your whole spirit and soul and body be preserved blameless unto the coming of our Lord Jesus Christ. Faithful is he that calleth you, who also will do it." I make the following observations concerning this promise:

a. According to Prof. Robinson's Lexicon, the language used here is the strongest form of expressing perfect or entire sanctification.

b. It is evident this is a prayer for and a promise of entire sanctification.

c. The very language shows that both the prayer and the promise refer to this life, since it is a prayer for the sanctification of the *body* as well as the soul; also that they might be *preserved*, not *after*, but *unto the coming of our Lord Jesus Christ*.

d. This is a prayer of inspiration coupled with an express promise that God will do it.

e. Its fulfillment, from the nature of the case, depends on our faith, since sanctification without faith is naturally impossible.

f. Now, if this promise, with those that have already been examined, does not, honestly interpreted, fully settle the question of the attainability of entire sanctification in this life, it is difficult to understand how *anything* can be settled by an appeal to Scripture.

There are many promises with the same significance to which I might refer you, and which if examined in the light of the foregoing rules of interpretation, would show tremendous evidence that sanctification is a doctrine of the Bible. Only examine them in the light of these plain self-evident principles and it seems to me that they cannot fail to produce conviction.

6

ENTIRE SANCTIFICATION IS ATTAINABLE

We must consider further why entire and permanent sanctification is attainable in this life and why its attainment must be an object of rational pursuit. I will now proceed to point out other reasons that support this doctrine:

1. *Christ prayed* for the entire sanctification of His followers in this life. "I pray not," He says, "that thou shouldest take them out of the world, but that thou shouldest keep them from the evil." He did not pray that they should be kept from persecutions or from natural death, but He clearly prayed that they should be kept from sin. Suppose Christ had commanded them to keep themselves from the evil of the world; what should we understand Him to mean by such a command?

2. Christ has taught us to pray for entire sanctification in this life; "Thy will be done in earth, as it is in heaven." Now, if there is entire sanctification in heaven, Christ requires us to pray for its existence on earth. And is it probable that He would have taught us to pray for that which He knows never can be or would be granted?

3. The Apostles evidently expected Christians to attain this state in this life. See Colossians 4:12: "Epaphras, who is one of you, a servant of Christ, saluteth you, always laboring fervently for you in prayers, that ye may stand perfect and complete in all the will of God." I make the following observations on this verse:

a. It was the object of the efforts of Epaphras—and a thing which he expected to bring about—to be instrumental in causing those Christians to be "perfect and complete in all the will of God."

b. If this language does not describe a state of entire sanctification, I know of none that would. If to be "perfect and complete in all the will of God" is not entire sanctification, what is?

c. Paul knew that Epaphras was laboring with expectation to this end; and he informed the Church of it in a manner that evidently showed his approval of the views and conduct of Epaphras.

4. It is further evident from 2 Corinthians 7:1 that the Apostles expected Christians to attain this state: "Having therefore these promises, dearly beloved, let us cleanse ourselves from all filthiness of the flesh and spirit, perfecting holiness in the fear of God."

Now, the Apostle speaks in this passage as if he really expected those to whom he wrote "to perfect holiness in the fear of God." Observe how strong and filled with meaning the language is, "Let us cleanse ourselves from all filthiness of the flesh and spirit." If "to cleanse ourselves from *all* filthiness of the *flesh*, and *all* filthiness of the *spirit*, and to perfect holiness" is not entire sanctification, what is? It is evident Paul expected this to take place in this life from the fact that he requires them to be cleansed from all filthiness of the *flesh* as well as of the spirit.

5. All the intermediate steps can be taken; therefore, the end can be reached. There is certainly no point in progressing toward entire sanctification if the intermediate steps are as far as we can go. Some have objected that though *all* the intermediate steps can be taken, yet the goal can never be reached in this life, just as five may be divided by three indefinitely without exhausting the fraction. Now this illustration deceives the mind that uses it, as it may the minds of those who listen to it. It is true that you can never exhaust the fraction in dividing five by three, for the plain reason that the division may be carried on indefinitely. There is no end! You cannot in this case

take all the intermediate steps, because they are infinite. But in the case of entire sanctification, all the intermediate steps can be taken. There is an end, or the state of entire sanctification, and that end is at a point infinitely short of infinite.

6. I argue that this state may be attained in this life from the fact that provision is made against all the occasions of sin. Men only sin when they are tempted, either by the world, the flesh, or the devil. And it is expressly asserted that in every temptation provision is made for our escape. Certainly, if it is possible for us to escape without sin, under every temptation, then a state of entire and permanent sanctification is attainable.

7. Full provision is made for overcoming the three great enemies of our souls: the world, the flesh, and the devil.

a. The world—"This is the victory that overcometh the world, even your faith. Who is he that overcometh the world, but he that believeth that Jesus is the Son of God?" (1 John 5:4, 5).

b. The flesh—"Walk in the Spirit, and ye shall not fulfil the lust of the flesh" (Gal. 5:16).

c. Satan—"The shield of faith. . .shall be able to quench all the fiery darts of the wicked" (Eph. 6:16). "And the God of peace shall bruise Satan under your feet shortly" (Rom. 16:20).

Now all sound rules of biblical criticism require us to understand the passages I have quoted in the sense I have quoted them.

8. It is evident from the following verses that abundant means are provided for the accomplishment of entire sanctification: "He that descended is the same also that ascended up far above all heavens, that he might fill all things. And he gave some, apostles; and some, prophets; and some, evangelists; and some, pastors and teachers; for the perfecting of the saints, for the work of the ministry, for the edifying of the body of Christ: till we all come in the unity of the faith, and of the knowledge of the Son of God, unto a perfect man, unto the measure of the stature of the fulness of Christ: that we henceforth be no more children, tossed to and fro, and carried about with every wind of doctrine, by the sleight of men, and cunning craftiness,

whereby they lie in wait to deceive; but speaking the truth in love, may grow up into him in all things, which is the head, even Christ: from whom the whole body fitly joined together and compacted by that which every joint supplieth, according to the effectual working in the measure of every part, maketh increase of the body unto the edifying of itself in love" (Eph. 4:10-16). Upon this passage I remark:

a. What is spoken of here is plainly applicable only to this life. It is in this life that the apostles, prophets, evangelists, pastors and teachers exercise their ministry. These means are applicable, therefore, so far as we know, only to this life.

b. In this passage, the Apostle clearly teaches that these means are designed for and are adequate for perfecting the whole Church as the body of Christ, "till we all come in the unity of the faith, and of the knowledge of the son of God, unto a perfect man, unto the measure of the stature of the fulness of Christ."

Now observe: These means are for the perfecting of the saints till the whole Church as a perfect man, has come to "the measure of the stature of the fulness of Christ." If this is not entire sanctification, what is? It is evident that this is to take place in this world from what follows: "That we henceforth be no more children, tossed to and fro, and carried about with every wind of doctrine, by the sleight of men, and cunning craftiness, whereby they lie in wait to deceive."

c. It should be observed that this is a very strong passage in support of the doctrine, since it asserts that abundant means are provided for the sanctification of the Church in this life. And since the whole includes all its parts, there must be sufficient provision for the sanctification of each individual.

d. If the work is ever to be accomplished, it is by these means. But these means are used only in this life. Entire sanctification, then, must take place in this life.

e. If this passage does not teach a state of entire sanctification, such a state is not mentioned anywhere in the Bible. And if in this passage believers are not said to be wholly sanctified by these means in this life, then I do not know where it is taught that they ever will be sanctified.

f. If this passage were put in the language of a command, how should we understand it? Suppose the saints are commanded to be perfect, and to grow up to "the measure of the stature of the fulness of Christ." Could anything less than entire sanctification be understood by such demands? By what rule of sound criticism can this language, used this way, mean anything less than what I have supposed it to mean?

9. God is able to perform this in and for us. Consider Ephesians 3:14-19: "For this cause I bow my knees unto the Father of our Lord Jesus Christ, of whom the whole family in heaven and earth is named, that he would grant you, according to the riches of his glory, to be strengthened with might by his Spirit in the inner man; that Christ may dwell in your hearts by faith; that ye, being rooted and grounded in love, may be able to comprehend with all saints what is the breadth, and length, and depth, and height; and to know the love of Christ, which passeth knowledge, that ye might be filled with all the fulness of God." I make the following observations on this passage:

a. Paul, evidently, is praying here for the entire sanctification of believers in this life. It is implied in our being "rooted and grounded in love," and being "filled with all the fulness of God," that we are to be as perfect in our measure and according to our capacity, as He is. If to be filled with the fulness of God does not imply a state of entire sanctification, what does?

b. Paul's statement in verse 20 shows that he did not see any difficulty in God's accomplishing this work in us: "Now unto him that is able to do exceeding abundantly above all that we ask or think, according to the power that worketh in us. . . ."

10. Nowhere does the Bible represent death as the termination of sin in Christians. Scripture could not neglect to tell us this, if it were true that Christians do not cease to sin until death. For a long time, it has been the custom of the Church to console individuals by telling them that death would terminate their struggle with all sin. This false notion has been used often in consoling the friends of deceased saints, to mention this as a most important fact: that now they had ceased from sin. However, if death is the termination of sin in the saints, and if they never cease to sin until they pass into eternity, why is the em-

phasis of that fact so utterly lacking. It seems utterly incredible that no inspired writer has ever noticed the fact. All the representations of Scripture are against this idea! It is said "Blessed are the dead which die in the Lord. . .that they may rest from their labors; and their works do follow them." This verse clearly teaches that they do not rest from their sins, but rather from their good works in this life. Their works that follow them do not curse but bless them. The teaching of Scripture is that death is the termination of the saint's suffering and labors of love *in this world* for the good of men and the glory of God. But nowhere in the Bible is it taught that the death of a saint is the termination of his serving the devil.

But, if it is true that Christians continue to sin till they die, and death is the one and only termination of their sin, then why is there so much Scriptural evidence to the contrary?

11. The Bible's teaching of death is totally inconsistent with the notion that it is an indispensable means of sanctification. In the Bible, death is represented as an enemy. But if death is the only condition upon which men are brought into a state of entire sanctification, then death is as important and as indispensable as the influence of the Holy Ghost. When death is represented in the Bible as anything else than an enemy, it is because it cuts short the sufferings of the saints, and introduces them into a state of eternal glory—not because it breaks them off from communion with the devil!

The contrast between the language of the Church and that of God's inspired Word on this subject is striking! The Church tries to console the Christian by telling him that death will terminate his sins—that he will then cease to serve the devil and his own lusts. The language of inspiration, on the other hand, is that he will cease, not from wicked, but from good works and labors and sufferings for God in this world. The language of the Church informs him, though mistakenly, that at death he will enter a life of unalterable holiness—that then, and not till then, will he be entirely sanctified. The language of inspiration, however, clearly teaches that *because he is sanctified*, death will usher him into a state of eternal glory.

12. Ministers of God are certainly bound to set up some

definite standard to which they must insist on complete conformity. My question is, What other standard can they and *dare* they set up than this? To insist on anything less than this is to twist Scripture and make an excuse for sin. But to set up this standard of sanctification, and then teach that it is impossible to attain in this life is sinning against God just as much as it would be to insist repentance in theory, and then avow that it was not attainable in practice.

And here let me ask Christians what they expect ministers to preach? Do you think they have a right to connive at any sin in you, or to insist upon anything else as a practicable fact than that you should abandon every iniquity? Sometimes, people say that we ministers preach too much on entire sanctification. But I would humbly ask what else can we preach? Is not every minister bound to insist in every sermon that men should wholly obey God? And because they will not compromise with any degree or form of sin, are they to be reproached for constantly preaching on the subject of entire obedience? I ask, By what authority can a minister preach anything less? And how shall any minister dare to teach the duty as a theory, and yet not insist on it as a practical matter, as something to be expected of every subject of God's kingdom?

13. A denial of this doctrine has the natural tendency to produce the very apathy which is now evident in the Church. Those who claim to be religious continue in sin without much conviction of its wickedness. Sin unblushingly stalks abroad even in the church of God and does not fill Christians with horror, because they expect its existence as a natural thing in this life. Tell a young convert that he must expect to backslide, and he will do so of course, and with comparatively little remorse, because he looks upon it as a kind of necessity. And being led to expect it, in a few months after his conversion you find him far from God and not the least bit horrified with his state.

In the same way, teach the idea among Christians that they are not expected to abandon all sin, and they will naturally continue in sin with the same indifference. Reprove them for their sins, and they will say, "Oh, we are imperfect creatures;

we do not pretend to be perfect, nor do we expect we ever will be in this world." Answers such as these will immediately show you the God-dishonoring and soul-ruining tendency of a denial of the doctrine of entire sanctification.

14. A denial of this doctrine causes ministers to make light of and pass over great iniquity in their churches. Having disbelieved this doctrine and feeling that a great amount of sin in all believers is to be expected as a thing of course, their whole preaching, spirit and conduct will only foster a high degree of apathy among Christians in regard to their abominable sins.

15. If this doctrine is not true, how profane and blasphemous is the covenant of every church of every evangelical denomination. Every church requires its members to make a solemn covenant with God, placing their hands on the emblems of the broken body and shed blood of the blessed Jesus, "to abstain from all ungodliness and every worldly lust, to live soberly and righteously in this present world." Now if the doctrine of the attainability of entire sanctification in this life is not true, this covenant is nothing more than profane mockery! It is a covenant made under the most solemn circumstances to live in a state of entire sanctification enforced by the most awful sanctions, and insisted on by the minister of God standing at the altar. Therefore, what right has any minister on earth to require less than this?

And again, what right does any minister have to require this, unless it is a practicable thing, something attainable in this life?

Suppose when this covenant was proposed to a convert about to unite with the church, he should take it to his closet, and spread it before the Lord, and pray whether it was right for him to make such a covenant—and whether the grace of the gospel can enable him to fulfill it.

Do you suppose the Lord Jesus would reply that if he made that covenant, he certainly would, and must as a matter of course habitually violate it as long as he lives, and that His grace was not sufficient to enable him to keep it? If that were the case, would he have any right to make the covenant? No, no more than he would have a right to lie.

16. Orthodox theologians have long maintained that a person who does not aim at living without sin is not a Christian—that unless he aims at perfection, he openly consents to live in sin; and is therefore certainly impenitent. It has been said, and I think truly, that if a man does not aim at total abstinence from sin in the fixed purpose of his heart, and aim at being wholly conformed to the will of God, he is not yet regenerated and does not mean to cease from abusing God.

Now if this is so, and I believe it certainly is, how can a person aim at and, indeed, do what he knows to be impossible? Is it not a contradiction to say that a man can intend to do what he knows he cannot do? The objection that some have raised to this is that; if it is true, it proves too much—it would prove that no one ever was a Christian who did not believe in this doctrine. To this I reply:

A man may believe in what is really a state of entire sanctification, and aim at attaining it, although he may not call it by that name. I believe this to be the case with Christians. They would attain what they aim at more frequently if they knew how to appropriate the grace of Christ to their own circumstances.

Christians commonly have supposed a state of entire consecration was attainable; but while they believe in physical depravity, they would not dare to call even entire consecration, entire sanctification. What is important is not what this state is called, but rather a firm appeal be insisted on with a clear explanation on the means of attaining it.

Call it what you please, Christian perfection, heavenly mindedness, or a state of entire consecration; by all these I understand the same thing. And it is certain that by whatever name it is called, the thing must be aimed at to be attained. The practicability of its attainment must be acknowledged or it cannot be aimed at. In fact, is not preaching anything short of this making provision for sin?

17. Another argument in favor of this doctrine is: the gospel as a matter of fact has often, not only temporarily but permanently and perfectly, overcome every form of sin in different individuals. Many have witnessed the power of the grace of God

slay completely and forever the most beastly lusts, drunkenness, lasciviousness and every other kind of long indulged and fully developed abomination. Now how was this done? It was accomplished by fully bringing this sin into the light of the gospel and showing the individual that in Christ's death the power of that sin was broken.

The only thing needed to slay any kind of sin is to help the mind fully grasp the truth of our baptism into the death of Christ and to see the effects of our own sins on the sufferings and agonies and death of our blessed Jesus. Let me state a fact to illustrate my meaning. A habitual smoker of tobacco whom I know, after having been presented with almost every argument to induce him to break the power of the habit and relinquish its use, in vain, on a certain occasion lighted his pipe, and was about to put it to his mouth, when the thought came to him, "did Christ die to free me from this vile indulgence?" He hesitated, but the thought persisted. "Did Christ die to free me from this vile indulgence?" As he realized the relation of the death of Christ to this sin, the power of that habit was instantly broken, and from that day on he has been free.

I could relate many other cases more amazing than this where a similar view of the relation of a particular sin to the atonement of Christ has in a moment not only broken the power of the habit, but destroyed entirely and forever the appetite for similar indulgences.

If the most deep-rooted habits of sin, and even those that involve physical consequences, and have deeply debased the body and rendered it a source of overpowering temptation to the mind, can be, and often have been utterly broken up and forever slain by the grace of God, why should it be doubted that by the same grace a man can triumph over all sin forever.

18. If this doctrine is not true, what is true on the subject? It is certainly very important that ministers be definite in their instructions. If Christians are not expected to be wholly conformed to the will of God in this life, then how much is expected of them? Who can say how far a person can go in his obedience? It is certainly absurd, not to say ridiculous, for ministers to continually press Christians on to higher and higher attain-

ments, saying at every step you can and must go higher, and yet all along informing them that they are expected to fall short of their whole duty—that they can as a matter of fact be better than they are, far better, indefinitely better; but still it is not expected that they will ever do their whole duty.

I have often been grieved to hear men preach who are afraid to commit themselves in favor of the whole truth; and who are yet evidently afraid of falling short in their instructions of insisting that men shall stand "perfect and complete in all the will of God." Because they are not fully persuaded that entire sanctification is possible in this life, there is no consistency in their views and teachings. If they do not teach that men ought to and are expected to do their whole duty, they are sadly at a loss to know what to teach. They evidently have many doubts about insisting upon less than this, and yet they still fear to preach the full extent of apostolic teaching on this subject. In their attempts to use qualifying terms and warnings, to avoid the impression that they believe in the doctrine of entire sanctification, they place themselves in a truly awkward position. Cases have occurred in which ministers have been asked, How far may we go, and how far are we expected to go, in depending upon the grace of Christ? How holy may men be, are expected to be, and must be, in this life? They could give no answer other than they can be a great deal better than they are. Now this indefiniteness is a great stumbling block to the Church. It does not concur with the teachings of the Holy Ghost.

19. The tendency of a denial of this doctrine is conclusive proof to my mind that the doctrine itself must be true. Many developments in the recent history of the Church throw light on this subject. It is plain to see that the facts developed in the temperance reformation have had a direct and powerful influence on this question. It has been ascertained that there is no possibility of completing the temperance reformation except by adopting the principle of total abstinence from all intoxicating drinks. Let a temperance lecturer go forth as an evangelist to promote revivals on the subject of temperance. Let him lecture against drunkenness while he admits and defends the moderate use of alcohol, or insinuates at least that total abstinence is not

expected or practicable. In this stage of the temperance reformation, every one can see that such a man could make no progress. He would be like a child building dams of sand to obstruct the rushing of mighty waters. It is as certain as causes produce their effects that no permanent reformation could be accomplished without adopting and insisting on the total abstinence principle.

Now if this is true respecting the temperance reformation, how much more so when applied to the subjects of holiness and sin. A man might by some possibility, even in his own strength, overcome his habits of drunkenness, and retain what might be called the temperate use of alcohol. But no such thing is possible in a reformation from sin. Sin is never overcome by any man in his own strength. If he acknowledges in his creed the necessity of any degree of sin, he becomes impenitent and consents to live in sin. He is abandoned by the Holy Spirit, and the certain result is relapsing into a state of legal bondage to sin. And this is probably a true history of ninety-nine one hundredths of the Church. It is exactly what might be expected because of the present faulty practice of the Church on this subject.

The reason for backsliding is that reformations are not carried deep enough. Christians are not set with all their hearts to aim at a speedy deliverance from all sin. On the contrary, they are left, and in many instances taught, to expect that they will sin as long as they live. When I was a young convert, I probably never will forget the effect produced on my mind by reading in the diary of David Brainerd that he never expected to make any considerable attainments in holiness in this life. I can now easily see this was a natural inference from the theory of physical depravity which he held. But not knowing this at the time, his viewpoint had a very injurious effect upon me for many years. It led me to reason thus: if such a man as David Brainerd did not expect to make much advancement in holiness in this life, it is vain for me to expect such a thing.

The fact is, if there is anything that is important to high attainments in holiness, and to the progress of the work of sanctification in this life, it is the adoption of the principle of total abstinence from sin. Total abstinence from sin must be every man's motto, or sin will certainly sweep him away as a flood. And I am fully convinced that until evangelists and pastors adopt and carry out in principle and practice the principle of total abstinence from *all* sin, they will certainly find themselves called to do their work over again every few months, as a temperance lecturer would who permits the moderate use of alcohol.

20. I reiterate, the tendency of the opposite view of this subject shows that that cannot be true. To call upon sinners to repent, and at the same time to inform them that they will not, and cannot, and are not expected to repent would forever prevent their repentance. Suppose you say to a sinner, "You are naturally able to repent; but it is certain that you never will repent in this life, either with or without the Holy Ghost." It is self-evident that such a teaching would only prevent his repentance. Likewise, say to a professor of religion, "You are naturally able to be wholly conformed to God; but it is certain that you never will be in this life, either in your own strength or by the grace of God." If this teaching is believed, it will just as certainly prevent his sanctification as the other teaching would the repentance of the sinner. I can speak from experience on this subject.

While I taught the common views, I was often instrumental in bringing Christians under great conviction, and into a state of temporary repentance and faith. But falling short of urging them up to a point where they would become so acquainted with Christ, as to abide in Him, they would, of course, soon relapse into their former state. I never saw, and can now understand that I had no reason to expect to see, under the instructions which I then gave, such a state of religious feeling, such steady and confirmed walking with God among Christians, as I have seen since I changed my views and instructions regarding entire sanctification.

7

ENTIRE SANCTIFICATION HAS BEEN ATTAINED

In final support of the attainability of entire sanctification in this life, I now would like to consider a very crucial question: have any actually attained the state of entire sanctification in this life? Some, who believe it is attainable, do not consider it of much importance to show that it has actually been attained. Now, I freely admit that it may be attainable, although it may never have been attained. Yet it appears to me that as a matter of encouragement to the Church, it would be very important to know if a state of entire and continued holiness has actually been attained by someone in this life. Since this question covers so much ground, I only intend to examine one case and see whether there is not reason to believe that in one instance, at least, it has been attained. The case to which I allude is that of the Apostle Paul. I propose to examine the passages that speak of him for the purpose of ascertaining whether there is evidence that he ever experienced this state in this life.

It seems plain to my mind that Paul and John, to say nothing of the other apostles, intended and expected the Church to understand them as speaking from personal experience, having received that fulness which they taught to be in Christ and in His gospel.

I would like to emphasize that I do not rest the practicability of attaining a state of entire and continued holiness at all upon whether anyone has ever attained it. Likewise, I certainly would not rest the question of whether the world ever will be converted upon the fact of whether it ever has been converted. When a factual case of attained entire holiness is urged as one argument among a great many to prove its attainability, and when used in this manner merely to encourage Christians to lay hold of this blessing, I have been surprised that objectors and reviewers fasten on this as the *doctrine* of sanctification, as if by calling this particular proof to question they could discredit all the other proof of its attainability. This is utterly absurd! Now, when I examine the character of Paul regarding this doctrine, if it does not appear clear to you that he did attain this state, you are not to overlook the fact that its attainability is already settled by other arguments on grounds entirely independent of practical experience. I merely use this as an argument simply because it appears to me to be a strong and appropriate one to instill great encouragement in Christians to press on after this blessing.

1. I will first mention some guidelines regarding the manner in which the language of Paul, when speaking of himself, should be understood; and then proceed to examine the passages which portray his Christian character.

a. His revealed character demands that we should understand him to mean all that he says when he speaks in his own favor.

b. The spirit of inspiration would guard him against speaking too highly of himself.

c. No man recorded ever seemed to possess greater modesty and feel more unwilling to exalt his own attainments.

d. If he considered himself as not having attained a state of entire sanctification, and as often, if not in all things, falling short of his duty, we may expect to find him acknowledging this in the deepest self-abasement.

e. If he is charged with living in sin, and with being wicked in anything, we may expect him, when speaking under inspiration, not to justify, but unequivocally to condemn himself in those things if he was really guilty.

2. Now in view of these facts, let us examine those scriptures in which he speaks of himself, and is spoken of by others as entirely sanctified.

a. 1 Thessalonians 2:10: "Ye are witnesses, and God also, how holily and justly and unblameably we behaved ourselves among you that believe." Upon this text I remark:

Here he unqualifiedly asserts his own holiness. This language is very strong, "How holily and justly and unblameably." If to be holy, just and unblamable is not entire sanctification, what is?

He appeals to the heart-searching God for the truth of what he says, and to their own observation. He calls on God, and on them also, to bear witness that he had been holy and without blame.

Here we have the testimony of an inspired Apostle, in the most unqualified language, asserting his own entire sanctification. Was he deceived? Can it be that he knew himself all the time to have been living in sin? If such language as this does not amount to an unqualified assertion that he had lived among them without sin, what can be known by the use of human language?

b. 2 Corinthians 6:3–7: "Giving no offense in any thing, that the ministry be not blamed: but in all things approving ourselves as the ministers of God, in much patience, in afflictions, in necessities, in distresses, in stripes, in imprisonments, in tumults, in labors, in watchings, in fastings; by pureness, by knowledge, by long-suffering, by kindness, by the Holy Ghost, by love unfeigned, by the word of truth, by the power of God, by the armor of righteousness on the right hand and on the left." Upon these verses I remark:

Paul asserts that he gave no offense in any thing, but in all things approved himself as a minister of God. Among other things he did this, "by pureness," "by the Holy Ghost," "by love unfeigned," and "by the armor of righteousness on the right hand and on the left." How could such a humble man as Paul speak of himself in this manner, unless he knew he was experiencing a state of entire sanctification and thought it very important that the Church should know it?

c. 2 Corinthians 1:12: "For our rejoicing is this, the testimony of our conscience, that in simplicity and godly sincerity, not with fleshly wisdom, but by the grace of God, we have had our conversation in the world, and more abundantly to you-ward." This passage plainly implies the same thing, and was clearly said for the same purpose—to declare the greatness of the grace of God as manifested in Paul's own life.

d. Acts 24:16: "And herein do I exercise myself, to have always a conscience void of offense toward God, and toward men." Paul, doubtless, at this time had an enlightened conscience. If an inspired Apostle could affirm that he exercised himself "to have always a conscience void of offense toward God, and toward men," must he not have been in a state of entire sanctification?

e. 2 Timothy 1:3: "I thank God, whom I serve from my forefathers with pure conscience, that without ceasing I have remembrance of thee in my prayers night and day." Here again he affirms that he serves God with a pure conscience. Could this be true, if he was violating his conscience often, and perhaps every day, as some suppose?

f. Galatians 2:20: "I am crucified with Christ: nevertheless I live; yet not I, but Christ liveth in me: and the life which I now live in the flesh, I live by the faith of the Son of God, who loved me, and gave himself for me." This does not assert that he lived without sin, but strongly implies it.

g. Galatians 6:14: "But God forbid that I should glory, save in the cross of our Lord Jesus Christ, by whom the world is crucified unto me, and I unto the world." This text also implies the same inference as above.

h. Philippians 1:21: "For to me to live is Christ, and to die is gain." Here the Apostle affirms that for him to live was as if Christ lived in the Church. How could he say this, unless his example and doctrine and spirit were those of Christ?

i. Acts 20:26: "Wherefore I take you to record this day, that I am pure from the blood of all men." This passage, taken in its context, clearly shows the impression Paul wanted to make on the minds of those to whom he spoke. It is certain that he could not be truly "pure from the blood of all men," unless he had done his whole duty. If he had been sinfully lacking in any grace, virtue, or labor, could he have said this? Certainly not!

j. 1 Corinthians 4:16, 17: "Wherefore I beseech you, be ye

followers of me. For this cause have I sent unto you Timotheus, who is my beloved son, and faithful in the Lord, who shall bring you into remembrance of my ways which be in Christ, as I teach every where in every church." Here Paul clearly set himself up as an example to the Church. How could he do this if he were living in sin? He sent Timotheus to them to refresh their memories in regard to his doctrine and *practice*; implying that what he taught in every church he himself practiced.

k. 1 Corinthians 11:1: "Be ye followers of me, even as I also am of Christ." Here Paul commands them to follow him, as he followed Christ; not so far as he followed Christ, as some seem to understand it, but to follow him because he followed Christ. How could he command the church to copy his example in this unqualified manner, unless he knew himself to be blameless?

l. Philippians 3:17, 20: "Brethren, be followers together of me, and mark them which walk so as ye have us for an ensample . . . For our conversation is in heaven; from whence also we look for the Savior, the Lord Jesus Christ." Here again, Paul calls upon the Church to follow him, and particularly to notice those that did copy his example, and points out the reason, "for our conversation is in heaven."

m. Philippians 4:9: "Those things, which ye have both learned, and received, and heard, and seen in me, do: and the God of peace shall be with you." The Philippians were commanded to do those things which they had learned, and received, and *seen* in him." And then he adds that if they *do* those things, the God of peace shall be with them. Now, can it be that he, Paul, meant that they should understand anything less than that he had lived without sin among them?

3. Next I will examine those passages which some assume to imply that Paul was not in a state of entire sanctification.

a. Acts 15:36–40: "And some days after Paul said unto Barnabas, Let us go again and visit our brethren in every city where we have preached the word of the Lord, and see how they do. And Barnabas determined to take with them John, whose surname was Mark. But Paul thought not good to take him with them, who departed from them from Pamphylia, and went not with them to the work. And the contention was so sharp between them, that they departed asunder one from the other: and so Barnabas took Mark, and sailed to Cyprus; and Paul chose Silas, and departed, being recommended by the brethren unto the grace of God."

This contention between Paul and Barnabas was founded upon the fact that John, who was a nephew of Barnabas, had once abruptly left them in their travels, it would seem, without any justifiable reason, and had returned home. It appears that Barnabas's confidence in his nephew was restored. Paul, however, was still not satisfied with the stability of his character and thought it dangerous to trust him as a traveling companion and fellow laborer. It is not intimated, nor can it be fairly inferred, that either of them sinned in this contention.

It sufficiently accounts for what occurred, to say they disagreed in their views of the expediency of taking John with them. Being men of principle, neither of them felt it his duty to yield to the opinion of the other. If either was to be blamed, it seems that Barnabas was at fault rather than Paul since he determined to take John with him without having consulted Paul. And he persisted in this determination until he met with such firm resistance on the part of Paul that he took John and sailed abruptly for Cyprus; while Paul choosing Silas, as his companion, was commended by the brethren to the grace of God and departed. Now certainly there is nothing in this transaction that Paul or any good man or an angel, under the circumstances, need to have been ashamed of that we can discover. In this instance, Paul was acting from a regard for the glory of God and the good of religion. And I would humbly question what kind of spirit finds sufficient evidence in this case to charge an inspired apostle with rebellion against God? But even admitting that he did sin in this case, where is the evidence that he was not afterward sanctified when he wrote the epistles— for this was before the writing of any of his epistles.

b. Acts 23:1–5: "And Paul, earnestly beholding the council, said, Men and brethren, I have lived in all good conscience before God until this day. And the high priest Ananias commanded them that stood by him to smite him on the mouth. Then said Paul unto him, God shall smite thee, thou whited wall: for sittest thou to judge me after the law, and commandest me to be smitten contrary to the law? And they that stood by said, Revilest thou God's high priest? Then said Paul, I wist not, brethren, that he was the high priest: for it is written, Thou shalt not speak evil of the ruler of thy people." In this case, sinful anger has been imputed to Paul, but so far as I can see, without any just reason. It seems plain that the contrary is to be inferred. It appears that Paul was not personally acquainted with the current high priest. And he manifested the utmost regard for the authority of God in quoting from the Old Testament, "Thou shalt not speak evil of the ruler of thy people"— implying that, notwithstanding the abuse he had received, he would not have made the reply had he known he was the high priest.

c. Many have supposed Romans 7:14–25 to be an epitome of Paul's experience at the time he wrote the epistle.

The context and drift of Paul's reasoning show that the case of which he was speaking, whether his own or the case of some one else, was cited by him to illustrate the influence of the law on the carnal mind. This is a case in which sin had entire dominion and overcame all his resolutions of obedience.

His use of the singular pronoun and in the first person proves nothing in regard to whether or not he was speaking of himself, for this is common with him and with other writers when using illustrations. He continues using the personal pronoun on into the eighth chapter. At the beginning, he represents himself or the person of whom he is speaking as being not only in a different, but in an exactly opposite state of mind. Now if the seventh chapter contains Paul's experience, whose experience is this in the eighth chapter? Are we to understand them both as the experience of Paul? If so, we must understand him as first speaking of his experience before and then after he was sanctified.

He begins the eighth chapter by saying, "There is therefore now no condemnation to them which are in Christ Jesus, who walk not after the flesh, but after the Spirit"; and points out as a reason, that "the law of the spirit of life in Christ Jesus hath made me free from the law of sin and death." The law of sin and death was that law in his members, or the influence of the flesh, of which he had so bitterly complained in the seventh chapter. But now it appears that he has passed into a state in which he is made free from this influence of the flesh, is emancipated and dead to the world and to the flesh, and in a state in which "there is no condemnation." Now if there was no condemnation in the state in which he was, it must have been, either because he did not sin; or, if he did sin, because the law of God was repealed or abrogated. If the penalty of the law was so set aside in his case, so that he could sin without condemnation, this is a real abrogation of the law. For a law without a penalty is no law, and if the law is set aside, there is no longer any standard, and he was neither sinful nor holy. But as the law was not and cannot be set aside, its penalty was not and cannot be abrogated so as not to condemn every sin. If Paul lived without condemnation, it must have been because he lived without sin.

It does not appear to me as if Paul speaks of his own experience in the seventh chapter of Romans, but that he merely supposes a case by way of illustration, and speaks in the first person and in the present tense simply because it was convenient and suitable to his purpose. His clear intention was to contrast the influence of the law and the gospel in the seventh and in the beginning of the eighth chapter. The seventh chapter describes the state of a man who was living in sin, condemned every day by the law, convicted and constantly struggling with his own corruptions, yet continually defeated by sin. The eighth chapter portrays a person enjoying gospel liberty, where the righteousness of the law is fulfilled in the heart by the grace of Christ. Clearly, the seventh chapter cannot apply to any who are in a state of entire sanctification.

I have already said that the seventh chapter contains the history of a person over whom sin has dominion. Now to assume that this was Paul's experience when he wrote the epistle, or of anyone who was experiencing the liberty of the gospel, is absurd and contrary to the experience of every person who has ever enjoyed gospel liberty. And further, this is totally contradicted in the sixth chapter. As I said, the seventh chapter portrays one over whom sin has dominion. But God says, in the sixth chapter of Romans in the fourteenth verse, "For sin shall not have dominion over you: for ye are not under the law, but under grace."*

I comment finally on this passage that if Paul was speaking of himself in the seventh chapter of Romans, and really giving a history of his own experience, it proves nothing at all in regard to his subsequent sanctification. If this was his experience at the time he wrote the epistle, it would prove nothing in regard to what occurred afterward in his own experience.

The eighth chapter shows conclusively that it was *not* his experience at the time he wrote the epistle. The fact that the seventh and eighth chapters have been separated since the translation was made, as I have said before, has led to much error in understanding this passage. Nothing is more certain than that the two chapters were intended to describe not only different experiences, but experiences opposite to each other. It is clearly impossible that both of these experiences could belong to the same person at the same time. If, therefore, Paul is speaking of his own experience in this context, we are bound to understand that at the time he wrote Romans, the seventh chapter described a former experience.

Now, if any one understands the seventh chapter as describing a Christian experience, he must understand it as describing one in a very imperfect state. The eighth chapter describes a soul in a state of entire sanctification. So Romans, instead of militating against the idea of Paul's entire sanctification on the supposition that he was speaking of himself, fully establishes the fact that he was actually in that state. What do those brethren mean who take the latter part of the seventh chapter as entirely disconnected with what precedes and follows it, and make it tell a sad story on the subject of the legal and sinful bondage of an inspired apostle? What cannot be proved from the Bible in this way? Is it not a sound and indispensable rule of biblical interpretation that a passage is to be taken in its

---

*See Finney's sermons on the seventh and eighth chapters of Romans in *Principles of Victory* and *Principles of Liberty*, published by Bethany House Publishers.

context, and that the scope and leading intention of the writer is to be continually kept in mind in deciding on the meaning of any passage? Why then are the verses that precede and those that immediately follow in the eighth chapter entirely overlooked in the examination of this important passage?

d. Philippians 3:10–15: "That I may know him, and the power of his resurrection, and the fellowship of his sufferings, being made conformable unto his death; if by any means I might attain unto the resurrection of the dead. Not as though I had already attained, either were already perfect: but I follow after, if that I may apprehend that for which also I am apprehended of Christ Jesus. Brethren, I count not myself to have apprehended: but this one thing I do, forgetting those things which are behind, and reaching forth unto those things which are before, I press toward the mark for the prize of the high calling of God in Christ Jesus. Let us therefore, as many as be perfect, be thus minded: and if in any thing ye be otherwise minded, God shall reveal even this unto you."

Here is a plain allusion to the Olympic games in which men ran for a prize, and were not crowned until the end of the race however well they might run.

Paul speaks of two kinds of perfection here; one he claims to have attained, and the other he had not. The perfection which he had not attained was that which he did not expect to attain until the end of his race, nor indeed until he had attained the resurrection from the dead. Until then he was not and did not expect to be perfect, in the sense that he should apprehend that for which he was apprehended of Christ Jesus. But all this does not imply that he was not living without sin, any more than it implies Christ was living in sin when He said, "I do cures today and tomorrow, and the third day I shall be perfected" (Luke 13:32). Here, Christ speaks of a perfection which He had not attained.

Now it is clear that it was the glorified state to which Paul had not attained—the perfection he was pressing after. But in the fifteenth verse, he speaks of another kind of perfection which he professed to have attained. "Let us therefore," he says, "as many as be perfect, be thus minded"; that is let us press after this high state of perfection in glory, "if by any means we may attain unto the resurrection of the dead." The figure of the games should be kept continually in mind in the interpretation of this passage. The prize in those races was the crown. This was given only at the end of the race. And besides, a man was "not crowned, except he strive lawfully"; that is, according to rules. Paul was running for the prize, the crown, not for entire sanctification, as some suppose, but for a crown of glory. He did not expect this until he had completed his race. He exhorts those who were perfect; that is, those who were running lawfully or according to rules, to forget the things that were behind and press toward the mark, toward the goal, toward the prize, or the crown of glory which the Lord, the righteous judge who was witnessing his race, would award to the victor on that day.

In this passage, Paul does not teach expressly or impliedly that he was living in sin, but the direct opposite. He meant to say, as he had said in many other places, that he was unblamable in respect to sin, and that he was aspiring after higher attainments and meant to be satisfied with nothing short of eternal glory.

4. Finally, in relation to the character of Paul, let me say:

a. If Paul was not sinless, he was an extravagant boaster. Such language used by any minister in these days would be considered as the language of an extravagant boaster.

b. If he were not in a state of entire sanctification, setting himself up as an example so often and fully without any caution or qualification was highly dangerous to the interests of the Church. It would be as wicked as it would be dangerous.

c. His language, in appealing to God that in his life and heart he was blameless, was blasphemous unless he was what he professed to be—entirely sanctified.

d. There is no reason for doubting his having attained this state. It dishonors God, therefore, to maintain that Paul had not attained the blessing of entire sanctification. Nowhere does he confess sin after he became an apostle, but invariably justifies himself, appealing to man and to God, for his entire integrity and blamelessness of heart and life.

e. To accuse him of sin in these circumstances, without evidence, is not only highly injurious to *him*, but disgraceful to the cause of religion.

f. To charge him with sin, when he claims to have been blameless, is to accuse him of falsehood or delusion.

g. To maintain the sinfulness of Paul is to deny the grace of the gospel and charge God foolishly. And I must inquire: why does this great effort to maintain that Paul lived in sin and was never wholly sanctified till death exist in the Church?

5. Two things have amazed me:

a. Many professed Christians seem to think they highly honor God in extending the claims of the law, and yet curtail and deny that the grace of the gospel is equal to the demands of the law.

Much has been said to the law's exceeding and infinite strictness, and the great length and breadth and height and depth of its claims. Many engage in defending the claims of the law, as if they greatly feared that the purity of the law should be defiled, its strictness and spirituality overlooked, and its high and holy claims set aside or brought down somehow to the level of human passion and selfishness. And while engaged in their zeal to defend the law, they talk and preach and write as if they supposed it indispensable in order to sustain the high claims of the law to deny the grace and power of the gospel and its sufficiency to enable human beings to comply with the requisitions of the law. Thus they seem to me, unwittingly to be among those who are against the grace of Christ, earnestly and vehemently denying that the grace of Christ is sufficient to overcome sin and fulfill in us the righteousness of the law. And in their zeal for the law, they appear to me either to overlook or flatly deny the grace of the gospel.

Now let the law be exalted. Let it be magnified and made honorable. Let the law be portrayed as strict, pure and perfect as its Author. Let it spread its claims over the whole realm of human and angelic accountability, and carry it like a blaze of fire to the deepest recess of every human heart. Exalt it as high as heaven, and thunder its authority and claims to the depths of hell. Stretch out its line upon the universe of mind. And let it, as it well may, and as it ought, thunder death and terrible damnation against every kind and degree of iniquity. Yet let it be remembered forever that the grace of the gospel is coextensive with the claims of the law.

Let no man, in his endeavor to maintain the authority of the law, insult the Savior, exercise unbelief himself, or dissipate and drown the faith of the Church by teaching the profane idea that the glorious gospel of the blessed God—made personal and rendered powerful by the efficacious application of the Holy Spirit—is not sufficient to fulfill in us "the righteousness of the law" and cause us "to stand perfect and complete in all the will of God."

b. The second thing which amazes me is so many seem to have an entirely self-righteous view of the doctrine of sanctification. They seem afraid to admit that any are entirely and perfectly sanctified in this life lest they flatter human pride. They seem to take it for granted that if any are entirely sanctified, they have something to glory in, as if they had done something and were in themselves better than others. Whereas, *the doctrine of entire sanctification utterly abhors the idea of human merit. It disclaims and repudiates human merit as a total abomination to God and to the sanctified soul. As taught in the Bible and as I understand it, this doctrine does not promote, in the least degree, the idea of anything naturally good in saints or sinners. It ascribes the whole of salvation and sanctification from first to last, not only till the soul is sanctified but at every moment while it remains in that state, to the indwelling Spirit and influence and grace of Christ.*

8

OBJECTIONS AND THEIR ANSWERS

In proceeding to answer some of the major objections to the doctrine of entire and continued sanctification in this life, I will begin with those passages of Scripture that are supposed to contradict it.

1. 1 Kings 8:46: "If they sin against thee, (for there is no man that sinneth not,) and thou be angry with them, and deliver them to the enemy, so that they carry them away captives unto the land of the enemy, far or near." My comments on this passage are:

a. This sentiment is repeated in nearly the same language in 2 Chronicles 6:26 and in Ecclesiastes 7:20, where the same original word in the same form is used.

b. These are the strongest passages I know of in the Old Testament and the same remarks are applicable to the three.

c. I will quote, for the satisfaction of the reader, the note of Dr. Adam Clarke on this passage, and also that of Barclay, the celebrated and highly spiritual author of "An Apology for the True Christian Divinity." They appear to me to be satisfactory answers to the objection founded on these passages.

CLARKE: *"If they sin against Thee.*—This must refer to some general defection from truth; to some species of false worship, idolatry, or corruption of the truth and ordinances of the Most High; as for it, they are here stated to *be delivered into the hands of their enemies, and carried away captive,* which was the general punishment of idolatry; and what is called, verse 47, *acting*

98

perversely, and *committing wickedness.*

"*If they sin against Thee, for* there is *no man that sinneth not.* The second clause, as it is here translated, renders the *supposition,* in the first clause, entirely nugatory; for, if there be *no man that sinneth not,* it is useless to say, IF *they sin:* but this contradiction is taken away by reference to the original *ki yechetau lak,* which should be translated, IF *they shall sin against Thee: or should they sin against Thee, ki ein adam asher lo yecheta;* 'For there is no man that *may* not sin:' that is, there is no man *impeccable,* none *infallible*; none that is not *liable* to transgress. This is the true meaning of the phrase in various parts of the Bible, and so our translators have understood the original; for, even in the thirty-first verse of this chapter, they have translated *yecheta,* IF *a man* TRESPASS; which certainly implies he *might* or *might not* do it: and in this way they have translated the same word, IF a *soul* SIN, in Leviticus 5:1, and 6:2; 1 Samuel 2:25; 2 Chronicles 6:22, and in several other places. The truth is, the Hebrew has no mood to express words in the *permissive* or *optative* way, but to express this sense it seems it uses the *future* tense of the conjugation *kal.*

"This text has been a wonderful strong-hold for all who believe that there is no redemption from sin in this life; that no man can live without committing sin; and that we cannot be entirely freed from it till we die.

"1. The text speaks no such doctrine, it only speaks of the *possibility* of every man's sinning; and this must be true of a state of *probation.*

"2. There is not another text in the divine records that is more to the purpose than this.

"3. The doctrine is flatly in opposition to the design of the gospel; for Jesus came to save his people from their sins, and to destroy the works of the devil.

"4. It is a dangerous and destructive doctrine, and should be blotted out of every Christian's creed. There are too many who are seeking to excuse their crimes by all means in their power; and we need not embody their excuses in a creed, to complete their deception, by stating that their sins are *unavoidable.*"

BARCLAY: "Secondly—another objection is from two passages of scripture, much of one signification. The one is 1 Kings 8:46: *for there is no man that sinneth not.* The other is Ecclesiastes 7:20: *for there is not a just man upon earth, that doeth good, and sinneth not.*

"I answer:

"1. These affirm nothing of a daily and continual *sinning*, so as never to be redeemed from it; but only that all have *sinned*, or that there is none that doth not *sin*, though not always, so as never to cease to *sin*; and in this lies the question. Yea, in that place of the Kings he speaks within two verses of the returning of such *with all their souls and hearts*; which implies a possibility of leaving off sin.

"2. There is a respect to be had to the seasons and dispensations; for if it should be granted that in Solomon's time there were none that *sinned not*, it will not follow that there are none such now, or that it is a thing not now attainable by the grace of God under the gospel.

"3. And lastly, This whole objection hangs upon a false interpretation; for the original Hebrew word may be read in the *potential mood*, thus, *there is no man who may not sin*, as well as in the *indicative*; so both the old Latin, Junius, and Tremellius, and Vatablus, have it; and the same word is so used, Psalm 119:11: *Thy Word have I hid in my heart, that I might not sin against Thee*, in the *potential mood*, and not in the *indicative*; which being more answerable to the universal scope of the scriptures, the testimony of the truth, and the sense of almost all interpreters, doubtless ought to be so understood, and the other *interpretation* rejected as *spurious*."

d. Whatever view may be taken concerning the views of these authors, I believe the preceding remarks are a plain and satisfactory answer to the objection founded on these passages. The objection might be true only under the Old Testament dispensation, and prove nothing in regard to the attainability of a state of entire sanctification under the New. What, does the New Testament dispensation differ nothing from the Old in its advantages for the acquisition of holiness? If it is true that no one attained a state of entire and permanent sanctification under the comparatively dark dispensation of Judaism, does that necessarily prove such a state is unattainable under the Gospel? It is plainly stated in the Epistle to the Hebrews that "the Old Covenant made nothing perfect, but the bringing in of a better hope did." Under the Old Covenant, God expressly promised that He would make a new one with the house of Israel in "writing the law in their hearts" and in "engraving it in their inward parts." And this New Covenant was to be made with the house of Israel under the Christian dispensation. What then do all such passages in the Old Testament prove in relation to the privileges and holiness of Christians under the New dispensation?

e. It is not my present intention to inquire whether any of the Old Testament saints did so far receive the New Covenant by way of anticipation, as to enter upon a state of entire and permanent sanctification. Nor will I, admitting that Solomon said in his day that "there is not a just man upon earth, that doeth good and sinneth not," inquire whether the same could with equal truth have been asserted of every generation under the Jewish dispensation.

f. The Bible says Abraham and multitudes of Old Testament saints "died in faith, not having received the promises." Now what can this mean? It cannot mean they did not know the promises, for the promises were made to them. It cannot mean that they did not receive Christ, for the Bible expressly asserts that they did—that Abraham rejoiced to see Christ's day (John 8:56).

Moses and all the Old Testament saints had so much knowledge of Christ as a Savior to be revealed that they were brought into a state of salvation. But still they did not receive the promise of the Spirit as it has been poured out under the Christian dispensation. The pouring out of the Spirit was the great thing promised all along, first to Abraham, or to his seed, which is Christ. Galatians 3:14, 16 states, "That the blessing of Abraham might come on the Gentiles through Jesus Christ; that we might receive the promise of the Spirit through faith. . .Now to Abraham and his seed were the promises made. He saith not, And to seeds, as of many; but as of one, And to thy seed, which is Christ."

The prophets promised this to the Christian Church: read Acts 2:16-21: "But this is that which was spoken by the prophet Joel; And it shall come to pass in the last days, saith God, I will pour out of my Spirit upon all flesh: and your sons and your daughters shall prophesy, and your young men shall see visions, and your old men shall dream dreams: and on my servants and on my handmaidens I will pour out in those days of my Spirit; and they shall prophesy: and I will show wonders in heaven above, and signs in the earth beneath; blood, and fire, and vapor of smoke: the sun shall be turned into darkness, and the moon into blood, before that great and notable day of the Lord come: and it shall come to pass, that whosoever shall call on the name of the Lord shall be saved." And in Acts 2:38, 39 we read: "Then Peter said unto them, Repent, and be baptized every one of you in the name of Jesus Christ for the remission of sins, and ye shall receive the gift of the Holy Ghost. For the promise is unto you, and to your children, and to all that are afar off, even as many as the Lord our God shall call." Also, Acts 3:24, 26 states, "Yea, and all the prophets from Samuel and those that follow after, as many as have spoken, have likewise foretold of these days . . . Unto you first God, having raised up his Son Jesus, sent him to bless you, in turning away every one of you from his iniquities."

Lastly, Christ himself promised, and He expressly styles *the promise* of the Father, Acts 1:4, 5: "And, being assembled together with them, commanded them that they should not depart from Jerusalem, but wait for the promise of the Father, which, saith he, ye have heard of me. For John truly baptized with water; but ye shall be baptized with the Holy Ghost not many days hence." The saints of the Old Testament times did not receive the light and the glory of the Christian dispensation nor the fulness of the Holy Spirit. And the Bible asserts that "they without us," that is, without our privileges, "should not be made perfect."

2. The next objection is founded on the Lord's Prayer. Christ taught us to pray, "Forgive us our debts, as we forgive our debtors." Some object that if a person should become entirely sanctified, he could no longer use this clause of this prayer, which

they say was clearly intended to be used by the Church to the end of time. Upon this prayer I remark:

a. Christ taught us to pray for entire and permanent sanctification. "Thy will be done on earth as it is done in heaven."

b. He expected us to pray believing that this prayer would be answered and that it was agreeable to His will.

c. The petition for forgiveness of our debts or trespasses, plainly must apply to past sins, and not to sins we are committing at the time we make the prayer. It would be absurd and abominable to pray for the forgiveness of a sin which we were then in the act of committing.

d. This prayer cannot properly be made in respect to any sin of which we have not repented. It would be highly abominable in the sight of God to pray for the forgiveness of a sin of which we did not repent.

e. If there is any hour or day in which a man has committed no actual sin, he could not consistently make this prayer in reference to that hour or that day. But,

f. At that time it would be highly proper for him to make this prayer in relation to all his past sins; although he may have repented of and confessed them and prayed for their forgiveness a thousand times before.

g. Although his sins may be forgiven, he still ought to feel penitent in view of them.

I am unable to see why this passage should be a stumbling block. If it is improper to pray for the forgiveness of past sins of which we have repented, then it is improper to pray for forgiveness at all. And if this prayer cannot be used suitably in reference to past sins of which we have already repented, it cannot properly be used at all, except on the absurd supposition that we are to pray for the forgiveness of sins which we are now committing and of which have not repented. And if it is improper to use this form of prayer in reference to all past sins of which we have repented, it is just as improper to use it in reference to sins committed today or yesterday of which we have repented.

3. Another objection is founded on James 3:1, 2: "My brethren, be not many masters, knowing that we shall receive the

greater condemnation. For in many things we offend all. If any man offend not in word, the same is a perfect man, and able also to bridle the whole body." Upon this passage I remark:

a. The term rendered "masters" may be rendered teachers, critics, or censors, and be understood either in a good or bad sense.* The Apostle exhorts the brethren not to be many masters, because if they are so they will incur the greater condemnation; "for," says he, "in many things we offend all." The fact that we all offend is here urged as a reason why we should not be many masters; which shows that the term masters is used in a bad sense here. "Be not many masters," for if we are masters, "we shall receive the greater condemnation," because we are all great offenders. Now I understand the following to be the simple meaning of this passage: do not many [or any] of you become censors, or critics, and set yourselves up to judge and condemn others. For in as much as you have all sinned yourselves, and we are all great offenders, we shall receive the greater condemnation if we set ourselves up as censors. "For with what judgment ye judge, ye shall be judged: and with what measure ye mete, it shall be measured to you again" (Matt. 7:2).

b. The Apostle is not affirming anything at all of the present character of himself or of those to whom he wrote. Nor is there the remotest allusion to the doctrine of entire sanctification. He simply affirms a well established truth in its application to a particular sin; that if they became censors, and injuriously condemned others, inasmuch as they had all committed many sins, they should receive the greater condemnation.

c. The Apostle did not intend to deny the doctrine of Christian perfection or entire sanctification, as I have explained them in this book, because he immediately adds, "If any man offend not in word, the same is a perfect man and able also to bridle the whole body."

4. Another objection is founded on 1 John 1:8: "If we say that we have no sin, we deceive ourselves, and the truth is not in us." Upon this I remark:

a. Those who make this passage an objection to the doctrine

---

*Most modern translations interpret "masters" as "teachers."

of entire sanctification in this life assume that the Apostle is speaking of sanctification instead of justification. But, it is evident that the Apostle makes no allusion here to sanctification. He is speaking solely of justification. A little attention to the context in which this verse stands will make this evident.

But before I proceed to state what I understand to be the meaning of this passage, let us consider it in its proper context, but in the sense in which they understand it who quote it for the purpose of opposing the doctrine of entire sanctification. They understand the Apostle as affirming that if we say we are in a state of entire sanctification and do not sin, we deceive ourselves and the truth is not in us. Now if this were the Apostle's meaning, he totally contradicts himself twice in the context.

b. This verse is immediately preceded by the assertion that "the blood of Jesus Christ cleanseth us from all sin." Now it would be very remarkable if immediately after this assertion the Apostle should mean to say (as they suppose he did) that it does not cleanse us from all sin, and if we say it does, we deceive ourselves. For he had just assumed that the blood of Jesus Christ *does* cleanse us from all sin. If this were his meaning, it implicates him in a very serious contradiction.

c. This view of the subject then represents the Apostle in the conclusion of the seventh verse as saying the blood of Jesus Christ His Son cleanseth us from all sin. And in the eighth verse as saying, if we suppose ourselves to be cleansed from all sin, we deceive ourselves, thus flatly contradicting what he had just said. And in the ninth verse he goes on to say that He is faithful and just to forgive us our sins, and to cleanse us from all unrighteousness; that is, the blood of Jesus Christ cleanses us from all sin. But if we say it does, we deceive ourselves. But if we confess our sins He is faithful and just to forgive us our sins and to cleanse us from all unrighteousness. Now, all unrighteousness is sin. If we are cleansed from all unrighteousness, we are cleansed from sin. And now suppose a man should confess his sin, and God should in faithfulness and justice forgive his sin and cleanse him from all unrighteousness, and then he should confess and profess that God had done this. Are we to understand that the Apostle would then affirm that he deceives himself in supposing that the blood of Jesus Christ cleanses him from all sin?

As I have already said, I do not understand the Apostle as affirming anything in respect to the present moral character of anyone, but as speaking of the doctrine of justification. In the tenth verse, he appears to affirm again what he had said in the eighth. If we say that we have not sinned, we make him a liar.

This, then, appears to me to be the meaning of the whole passage. If we say that we are not sinners, that is, say we have no sin and no need of the blood of Christ, and that we have never sinned and consequently need no Savior, we deceive ourselves. For we have sinned, and nothing but the blood of Christ cleanses us from sin or procures our pardon and justification. If we will not deny but confess that we have sinned, "He is faithful and just to forgive us our sins, and to cleanse us from all unrighteousness." "But if we say that we have not sinned, we make him a liar, and his word is not in us."

5. It has been objected to the view I have given of Jeremiah 31:31-34, saying that if that passage is to be considered as a promise of entire sanctification, this proves too much. Since it says, "they shall all know the Lord from the least to the greatest," the objector says it would prove that all the Church has been in a state of entire sanctification ever since the commencement of the New Testament dispensation. To this objection I answer:

a. I have already shown that this promise is conditioned on faith, and that the blessing cannot possibly be received except by faith.

b. It is absolutely certain that many have received this covenant in its fullness.

c. A promise may be unconditioned or absolute, and certain of a fulfillment in relation to the whole Church as a body in some period of its history, which is nevertheless conditional in relation to its application to any particular individuals or generation.

d. I think it is entirely faithful to the prophecies to understand this passage as expressly promising to the Church a day when all her members shall be sanctified, and when "upon the bells of the horses, Holiness unto the Lord" shall be written. It appears to be abundantly foretold that the Church as a body will enter into a state of entire sanctification in some period of her history in this world; and that this will be the carrying out of these promises of the New Covenant of which we are speaking. But it is by no means an objection to this view of the subject that all the Church has not yet entered into this state.

e. Some maintain that this promise in Jeremiah has been fulfilled already. This has been argued, from the fact that the promise has no condition expressed or implied, and the responsibility therefore rests with God. They say the Apostle, in his epistle to the Hebrews, quotes it as meaning it was fulfilled at the coming of Christ. Now to this I answer:

It might as well be argued that all the rest of the promises and prophecies relating to the gospel day were fulfilled, because the time had come when the promise was due. Suppose it were denied that the world would ever be converted, or that there ever would be any more piety in the world than there has been and is at present. Suppose the promises and prophecies respecting the latter day glory and the conversion of the world should be cited as proof that the world is to be converted, and some replied that these promises had already been fulfilled—that they were unconditional—and that the coming of the Messiah was the time when they became due.

Suppose in reply it is emphasized that nothing has ever yet occurred in the history of this world that seems at all to have fulfilled the meaning of these promises and prophecies—that the world has never been in the state which seems to be plainly described in these promises and prophecies. And further, it is argued that the world has not yet experienced what is meant by the Bible in relation to the future state of the world.

Now suppose in reply it is argued that we are to interpret the language of the promises and prophecies by the fact that since the promises and prophecies were unconditional, and the gospel day has really come when they were to be fulfilled, we certainly know, whatever their language may be, that they meant nothing more than what the world has already realized?

This would be precisely like the reasoning of some persons in relation to Jeremiah 31:31-34:

They say, the promises are without condition. And, the time has come for their fulfillment. Therefore, the world has realized their fulfillment and all that was intended by them.

They reason that the facts in the case settle the question of context and interpretation: and that we know that they never intended to promise a state of entire sanctification, because, as a matter of fact, no such state has been realized by the Church. If this kind of reasoning is valid, then the Bible is the most exaggerated, if not ridiculous, book in the universe.

If what the world has seen in regard to the extension and universal prevalence of the Redeemer's kingdom is all that the promises relating to these events really mean, then the Bible, of all books in the world, is the most apt to deceive mankind. But who, after all, can honestly agree with this kind of reasoning? Who does not know, or may not know if he will use his common sense, that although these promises and prophecies are unconditionally expressed; yet, they are as a matter of fact really conditioned on a right exercise of human agency, and that a time is to come when the world shall be converted. The conversion of the world implies in itself a vastly higher state of religious feeling and action in the Church than has for centuries, or perhaps ever, been witnessed. The promise of the New Covenant is still to be fulfilled in a higher sense than it ever has been. If any man doubts this, I must believe that he does not truly understand his Bible.

I insist that faith is an indispensable condition for the fulfillment of all promises of spiritual blessings, to be received by the exercise of our human powers.

Some, who hold the confused views mentioned above, *imagine* that they see a very close connection, if not an absolute identity, of our views with those of modern Antinomian Perfectionists. But like themselves, the Antinomian Perfectionists insist that these are promises without condition, and that consequently their own watchfulness, prayers, exertions, and the right exercise of their own agency are not at all to be taken into account in the matter of their perseverance in holiness. They throw the responsibility entirely upon Christ, since they interpret promises as without condition. The thing that He has promised, they say, is that He will keep them in a state of entire sanctification without any condition. Therefore, for them to confess sin is to accuse Christ of breaking His promises. For them to make any efforts at perseverance in holiness is to set aside the gospel and go back to the law. For them even to fear that they will sin is to fear that Christ will tell a lie.

This, and their setting aside of the moral law, are two great errors of their whole system. It would be easy to show that the adoption of this view—that these promises are without condition expressed or implied—has led to some of the most fanatical and absurd opinions and practices. They take the ground that no condition is expressed, and therefore, none is implied. They overlook the fact that the very nature of the thing promised implies that faith is the condition on which its fulfillment must depend. It is hoped, therefore, that these brethren who charge us with perfectionism will be led to see that they are guilty of Antinomian Perfectionism and not us.

These are the principle passages from Scripture that I believe those who oppose the doctrine of entire sanctification lay the most stress on. In the next chapters, I will answer more objections that may seem to be of weight. This I intend to do without either the spirit or the form of controversy.

9

ERRORS OF PERFECTIONISTS

There are many objections to the doctrine of entire sanctification besides those derived from the passages of Scripture
which I have already considered. Some of these objections are
doubtless honestly felt and deserve to be considered. I will now
proceed to point out some of them.

1. Some object that the doctrine of entire and permanent
sanctification in this life *tends* to the errors of modern perfectionism. This objection has been honestly set forth by some good
men. But still I cannot believe that they have really considered
the matter. I believe one fact will set aside this objection. It is
well known that the Wesleyan Methodists have, as a denomination from the earliest period of their history, maintained this
doctrine in all its entirety. Now if such is the tendency of the
doctrine, it is very strange that this tendency has never developed itself in that denomination. So far as I can learn, the Methodists have been in a great measure, if not entirely, exempt
from the errors held by modern perfectionists. Perfectionists,
as a whole and I believe with very few exceptions, have arisen
out of those denominations that deny the doctrine of entire
sanctification in this life.

Now the reason for this is obvious to my mind. When those
who profess to be religious, who have been subject to bondage
all their life, begin to inquire earnestly for deliverance from
their sins, they have found neither sympathy nor instruction
in regard to the prospect of getting rid of them in this life. Then

they have gone to the Bible, and there found in almost every part of it Christ presented as a Savior from their sins. But when they proclaim this truth, they are at once treated as heretics and fanatics by their brethren, until, being overcome of evil, they fall into censoriousness. Finding the Church so decidedly and utterly wrong in her opposition to this one great important truth, they lose confidence in their ministers and the Church, and being influenced by a wrong spirit, Satan takes advantage of them and drives them to the extreme of error and delusion. I believe this is the true history of many of the most pious members of the Calvinistic churches.

On the contrary, the Methodists are very much protected against these errors. They are taught that Jesus Christ is a Savior from all sin in this world. And when they inquire for deliverance, they are pointed to Jesus Christ as a present and all-sufficient Redeemer. Finding sympathy and instruction on this great and agonizing point, their confidence in their ministers and their brethren remains and they maintain proper relationships with them.

It seems impossible to me that the tendency of this doctrine should lean toward the peculiar errors of the modern perfectionists, and yet not an instance has occurred among all the Methodist ministers, or the thousands of their members, for one hundred years.

Let me say that I am fully convinced that there are only two ways in which present-day ministers can prevent members of their churches from becoming perfectionists. One is to let them live so far from God that they will not inquire after holiness of heart; and the other is to fully teach the glorious doctrine of entire consecration, and that it is the high privilege as well as the duty of Christians to live in a state of entire consecration to God in this life.

I can say from my own experience that since I have understood and fully taught the doctrine as I now hold it, I see no tendency to these errors among those who listen to my instructions. In churches not far distant, where the doctrine which we teach here is opposed, there seems to be a constant tendency among their most pious people toward Antinomian Perfectionism. How can this be accounted for on any other principle than the one stated above? I can truly say that those persons here, who have been the first to lay hold of the doctrine of entire sanctification in this life, and who give the highest evidence of enjoying the blessing of present sanctification, have been far removed from the errors of the modern perfectionists.

Aside from the facts, what is the foundation of all the errors of the modern perfectionist? Everyone who has examined them knows that they may be summed up in this: the abrogation of the moral law. And now I would humbly inquire, What possible tendency can there be to their errors if the moral law is preserved in the system of truth? In these days everyone knows, that the "head and front of their offending" and falling is the setting aside of the law of God. The setting aside of the Christian ordinances of baptism and the Lord's Supper originates out of the same principle and manifestly grows out of the abrogation of the law of God. But retain the law of God, as the Methodists have done and as other denominations have done who from the days of the Reformation have maintained this same doctrine, and there is certainly no tendency to Antinomian Perfectionism.

I have many things to say about the tendency of this doctrine, but at present this must suffice.

Attempts are made to show in what particulars Antinomian Perfectionism and our views are the same. On this I remark:

a. Instead of meeting a proposition in the open field of fair and Christian debate, it seems for a long time to have been a favorite policy of certain controversial writers to try to give it a bad name and attempt to put it down not by force of argument, but by showing that it is identical with or sustains a near relation to Pelagianism, Antinomianism, Calvinism, or some other *ism*, against which certain classes of minds are deeply prejudiced.

In the recent controversy between what are called Old and New School theologians, who has not witnessed with pain the frequent attempts that have been made to put down the New School Divinity, as it is called, by calling it Pelagianism and quoting certain passages from Pelagius and other writers to show the identity of sentiment that exists between them?

This is a very unsatisfactory method of attacking or defending any doctrine. There are, no doubt, many points of agreement between Pelagius and all truly orthodox theologians, as well as many points of disagreement. There are also many points of agreement between modern perfectionists and all Evangelical Christians, and so there are many points of disagreement between them and the Christian Church in general. That there are some points of agreement between their views and my own is no doubt true. And that we totally disagree in regard to those points that constitute their great peculiarities, is, if I understand them, also true.

But even if I did really agree in all points with Augustine or Edwards, or Pelagius, or the modern perfectionists, neither the good nor the ill name of any of these would prove my point of views to be either right or wrong. It would remain, after all, to show that those with whom I agreed were either right or wrong, in order on the one hand to establish that for which I contend, or on the other to overthrow that which I maintain. It is often more convenient to give a doctrine or an argument a bad name, than it is soberly and satisfactorily to reply to it.

b. I find it a little strange we should be charged with holding the same point of views as the perfectionists. They seem to be more violently opposed to our views, since they have come to understand them, than almost any other persons whatever. I have been informed by one of their leaders that he regards me as one of the master-builders of Babylon. And I also understand that they manifest greater hostility to the *Oberlin Evangelist* than almost any other class of persons.

c. I will not take time, nor is it needful, to go into an investigation or a denial of the supposed or alleged points of agreement between us and the perfectionists. But for the present it must be sufficient to request you to read and examine for yourselves.

With respect to the modern perfectionists, those who have been acquainted with their writings know that some of them have strayed much further from the truth than others. Some of their leading men, who began with them and adopted their name, stopped far short of adopting some of their most abominable errors. Still maintaining the authority and perpetual obligation of the moral law, they have been saved from falling into many of the most objectionable and destructive notions of the sect. There are many more points of agreement between that class of perfectionists and the orthodox church than between any other class of them and the Christian Church. And there are still a number of important points of difference, as everyone knows who has correct information on this subject.

I abhor the practice of denouncing whole classes of men for the errors of some of that name. I am well aware that there are many of those who are termed "Perfectionists," who as truly abhor the extremes of error into which many of that name have fallen as perhaps do any persons living.

2. Others object that persons could not live in this world if they were entirely sanctified. Strange! Does holiness injure a man? Does perfect conformity to all the laws of life and health, both physical and moral, render it impossible for a man to live? If a man stops rebelling against God, will it kill him? Does there appear to have been anything in Christ's holiness inconsistent with life and health? This objection is founded on a gross mistake in regard to what constitutes entire sanctification. They suppose that this state implies a continual and very intense degree of excitement, and many of those things which I have shown in a former part of this discourse are not at all implied in it. I have thought that it is a *glorified* rather than a *sanctified* state that most men have before their minds whenever they consider this subject. When Christ was on earth, He was in a sanctified but not in a glorified state. "It is enough for the disciple that he be as his master" (Matt. 10:25). Now what is there in the moral character of Jesus Christ, as represented in His history, aside from His miraculous powers, that may not and ought not be fully copied in the life of every Christian? I speak not of His knowledge, but of His spirit and temper. Ponder well every circumstance of His life that has come down to us, and say, "Beloved, what is there in it, that may not, by the grace of God, be copied in your own? And do you think that a full imitation of Him in all that relates to His moral character would

render it impossible for you to live in this world?"

3. Again, some object against our professing a state of entire sanctification because they believe it not only implies present obedience to the law of God, but such a formation and perfection of holy habits as to render it certain that we shall never again sin. And further, that a man can no more tell when he is entirely sanctified, than he can tell how many holy acts it will take him to form holy habits of such strength that he will never sin again. To this I answer:

a. The law of God has nothing to do with requiring this formation of holy habits. The law of God is satisfied with present obedience, and only demands at every present moment the full devotion of all our powers to God. It never in any instance complains that we have not formed such holy habits that we shall sin no more.

b. If it is true that a man is not entirely sanctified until his holy habits are fixed as to render it certain that he will never sin again, then Adam was not in a state of entire sanctification previous to the fall, nor were the angels in this state before their fall.

c. If this objection is true, there is not a saint nor an angel in heaven, so far as we can know, that can with the least propriety profess a state of entire sanctification. For, how can they know that they have performed so many holy acts as to have created such habits of holiness as to render it certain that they will never sin again?

d. Entire and continued sanctification does not depend upon the formation of holy habits, nor at all consist in this. But both entire and permanent sanctification are based alone upon the grace of God in Jesus Christ. Perseverance in holiness is to be ascribed entirely to the influence of the indwelling Spirit of Christ, both now and to the end of our lives, instead of being secured at all by any habits of holiness which we may or ever shall have formed.

4. Another objection is that the doctrine tends to spiritual pride. And is it true, indeed, that to become perfectly humble tends to pride? But entire humility is implied in entire sanctification. Is it true that you must remain in sin, and of course

cherish pride, in order to avoid pride? Is your humility more safe in your own hands? Are you more secure against spiritual pride in refusing to receive Christ as your Helper, than you would be in embracing Him at once as a full Savior?

5. Again it is objected that many who have embraced this doctrine really are spiritually proud. To answer this I call attention to the many who have believed in the doctrine of regeneration and have been deceived and amazingly puffed up with the idea that they have been regenerated when they have not. Is this a good reason for abandoning the doctrine of regeneration, or any reason why the doctrine should not be preached?

Let me inquire, Has not a simple declaration of what God has done for their souls been *assumed* as itself sufficient evidence of spiritual pride on the part of those who embrace this doctrine, while in reality there was no spiritual pride at all? It seems next to impossible, with the present views of the Church, that an individual should really attain this state and profess it in a manner so humble as not of course to be suspected of enormous spiritual pride. This consideration has been a snare to some who have hesitated and even neglected to declare what God had done for their souls, lest they should be accused of spiritual pride. And this has been a serious injury to their piety.

6. But again it is objected that this doctrine tends to censoriousness. Undeniably, some who have professed to believe in this doctrine have become censorious. But this no more condemns this doctrine than it condemns that of regeneration. And that it tends to censoriousness might just as well be urged against every acknowledged doctrine of the Bible as against this doctrine.

Let any Christian do his whole duty to the Church and the world in their present state—let him speak to them and of them as they really are—and he would of course incur the charge of censoriousness. It is, therefore, the most unreasonable thing in the world to suppose that the Church, in its present state, would not accuse any perfect Christian of censoriousness. Entire sanctification implies the doing of all our duty. But to do all our duty we must rebuke sin in high places and in low places. Can this be done with all needed severity without, in many cases, giving offense and incurring the charge of censoriousness? No; it is impossible; and to maintain the contrary would be to impeach the wisdom and holiness of Jesus Christ himself.

7. It is objected that this doctrine lowers the standard of holiness to a level with our own experience. It is not denied that in some instances this may have been true. Nor can it be denied that the standard of Christian perfection has been elevated much above the demands of the law in its application to human beings in our present state of existence. Some have forgotten that the inquiry is, What does the law demand—not of angels and what would be entire sanctification of them; nor of Adam previous to the fall when his powers of body and mind were all in a state of perfect health; not what the law will demand of us in a future state of existence; not what the law may demand of the Church in some future period of its history on earth when the human constitution by the universal prevalence of correct and thorough temperance principles may have acquired its pristine health and power—but the question, What does the law of God require of Christians of the present generation; of Christians in all respects in our circumstances, with all the ignorance and debility of body and mind which have resulted from the intemperance and abuse of the human constitution through so many generations?

The law levels its claims to us as we are, and a just exposition of it, as I have already said, under all the present circumstances of our being, is indispensable to a right apprehension of what constitutes entire sanctification.

To be sure, there may be danger of frittering away the claims of the law and letting down the standard. But I would humbly inquire whether, hitherto, the error has been on the other side: Whether as a general fact the law has not been so interpreted as to naturally beget the idea so prevalent that if a man should become holy he could not live in this world?

In a letter from a beloved and useful and venerated minister of the gospel, the writer expressed the greatest attachment to the doctrine of entire consecration to God, and said that he preached the same doctrine which we hold to his people every Sabbath, *but by another name*. Still he added that it was revolting to his feelings to hear any mere man set up the claim of obedience to the law of God. Now let me inquire, Why should this be revolting to the feelings of piety? Must it not be because the law of God is supposed to require something of human beings in our state which it does not and cannot require? Why should such a claim be thought extravagant, unless the claims of the living God be thought extravagant? If the law of God really requires no more of men than what is reasonable and possible, why should it be revolting to any mind to hear an individual profess to have attained to entire obedience? I know that the brother to whom I allude would be almost the last man to deliberately and knowingly give any strained interpretation to the law of God; and yet, I cannot but feel that much of the difficulty that good men have with this subject has arisen out of a comparison of the lives of saints with a standard entirely above that which the law of God does or can demand of persons in all respects in our circumstances.

8. Another objection is that the grace of God is not sufficient to secure the entire sanctification of saints in this life. Some maintain that the question of the attainability of entire sanctification in this life can be summed up into one question: Is the Church and are Christians sanctified in this life? The objectors say that nothing is sufficient grace that does not clearly secure the faith and obedience and perfection of the saints; and therefore, that the provisions of the gospel are in fact to be measured by the results, and that the experience of the Church decides both the meaning of the promises and the extent of the provisions of grace. Now to this I answer:

If this objection is good for anything in regard to entire sanctification, it is equally true in regard to the spiritual state of every person in the world. If the fact that men are not perfect proves that no provision is made for their perfection, their being no better than they are proves that there is no provision for their being any better than they are, or that they might have aimed at being any better with any rational hope of success. But who, except a fatalist, will admit any such conclusion as this? And yet this conclusion is inevitable from such premises.

9. Another objection to this doctrine is that it is contrary

to the views of some of the greatest and best men in the Church. Such men as Augustine, Calvin, Doddridge, Edwards, etc., were of a different opinion. To this I answer:

Suppose they were; we are not to call any man father in such a sense as to allow him to form our views of Christian doctrine.

This objection comes with a very ill grace from those who wholly reject the opinions of these men on some of the most important points of Christian doctrine.

These men all held the doctrine of physical depravity, and this is why they rejected the doctrine of entire consecration to God in this life. Maintaining, as they seem to have done, that the constitutional sensitivities of body and mind were depraved and *sinful*, consistency of course led them to reject the idea that persons could be entirely sanctified while in the body. Now I would ask, What consistency is there in quoting them as rejecting the doctrine of entire sanctification in this life, while the reason of this rejection in their minds was founded in the doctrine of physical depravity, which notion is entirely denied by those who quote their authority?

10

KNOWING YOUR RELATIONSHIP WITH GOD

In this chapter, as in the previous one, I will continue to answer seriously intended objections as they deserve appropriate consideration. The first and primary one is leveled against being conscious of a state of entire sanctification.

1. Some object that if we should ever attain this state of entire and continual consecration or sanctification, we could not know it until the day of Judgment, and that to maintain its attainability is vain, since no one can know whether he has attained it or not. To this I reply:

a. A man's consciousness is the highest and best evidence of the present state of his own mind. I understand consciousness to be the mind's recognition of its own states, and that it is the highest possible evidence to our own minds of what transpires within us. Consciousness can, of course, testify only to our present sanctification, but with the law of God before us as our standard, the testimony of our consciousness in regard to whether our mind is conformed to that standard or not is the highest evidence which the mind can have of a present state of conformity to that rule.

It is a testimony which we cannot doubt any more than we can doubt our existence. How do we know that we exist? I answer: by our consciousness. How do I know that I breathe or love or hate or sit or stand or lie down or rise up—that I am joyful or sorrowful—in short, that I exercise any emotion or volition or affection of mind? How do I know that I sin or repent or believe? I answer: by my own consciousness. No testimony can be so direct and convincing as this.

Now in order to know that my repentance is genuine, I must intellectually understand what genuine repentance is. So if I would know whether my love to God or man, or obedience to the law, is genuine, I must clearly understand the real spirit, meaning, and bearing of the law of God. Having the rule before my mind, my own consciousness affords the most direct and convincing evidence possible of whether my present state of mind is conformed to the rule.

The Spirit of God is never employed in testifying to what my consciousness teaches, but in setting in a strong light before the mind the rule to which I am to conform my life. It is His business to make me understand, to induce me to love and obey the truth; and it is the business of consciousness to testify to my own mind whether I do or do not obey the truth when I apprehend it. A man may be mistaken in regard to the correctness of the law or truth of God. He may therefore mistake the character of his exercises. But when God so presents the truth as to give the mind assurance that it understands His mind and will upon any subject, the mind's consciousness of its own exercise in view of that truth is the highest and most direct possible evidence of whether it obeys or disobeys.

If a man cannot be conscious of the character of his own exercises, how can he know when and of what he is to repent? If he has committed sin of which he is not conscious, how is he to repent of it? And if he has a holiness of which he is not conscious, how could he feel that he has peace with God?

Some say a man may violate the law not knowing it, and consequently have no consciousness that he sinned; then afterward a knowledge of the law may convict him of sin. However, if there was absolutely *no* knowledge that the thing in question was wrong, the doing of that thing was not sin, since some degree of knowledge of what is right or wrong is *indispensable* to the moral character of any act. In such a case, there may be a sinful ignorance which may involve all the guilt of those actions that were done in consequence of it; but that blameworthiness lies in the ignorance itself, and not at all in the violation of the rule of which the mind was at the time entirely ignorant.

The Bible everywhere assumes that we are able to know, and unqualifiedly requires us to know, what the moral state of our mind is. It commands us to examine ourselves, to know and to prove our own selves. Now how can this be done, but by bringing our hearts into the light of the law of God, and then taking the testimony of our own consciousness, whether we are or are not in a state of conformity to the law? But if we do not receive the testimony of our consciousness in regard to our sanctification, do we receive it in respect to our repentance or any other exercise of our mind whatever? The fact is that we may deceive ourselves by neglecting to compare ourselves with the right standard. But when our views of the standard are right, and our consciousness is a felt, decided, unequivocal state of mind, we cannot be deceived any more than we can be deceived in regard to our own existence.

b. But it is said our consciousness does not teach us what the power and capacities of our minds are, and that therefore, if consciousness could teach us in respect to the *kind* of our exercises, it cannot teach us in regard to their *degree*, whether they are equal to the present capability of our mind. I would answer that consciousness does as unequivocally testify of whether we do or do not love Him at all. How does a man know that he lifts as much as he can or runs or leaps or walks as fast as he is able? I answer: by his own consciousness. How does he know that he repents or loves with all his heart? Again I answer: by his own consciousness. This is the only possible way in which he can know it.

The objection implies that God has not put within our reach any possible means of knowing whether we obey Him or not. The Bible does not *directly* reveal to any man the fact of whether he obeys God or not. It reveals his duty, but does not reveal the fact of whether he obeys. It refers this testimony to his own consciousness. The Spirit of God sets our duty before us, but does not directly reveal to us whether we do it or not: for this would imply that every man is under constant inspiration.

But some say the Bible directs our attention to the fact of

whether we obey or disobey as evidence of whether we are in a right state of mind or not. But I would inquire, how do we know whether we obey or disobey? How do we know anything of our conduct but by our consciousness? Our *conduct* as observed by others is to them evidence of the state of our hearts. But, I repeat it, our *consciousness* of obedience to God is to us the highest and, indeed, the only evidence of our true character.

If a man's own consciousness is not to be a witness either for or against him, no other testimony in the universe can ever satisfy him of the propriety of God's dealing with him in the final Judgment. Even if ten thousand witnesses testify that a man has committed murder, still the man could not feel condemned for it unless his own consciousness bore testimony to the fact. On the other hand, if ten thousand witnesses should testify that he has performed some good act, he could feel no self-complacency, or sense of self-approbation and virtue unless his consciousness bore its testimony to the same fact.

There often are cases where the witnesses testify to the guilt or innocence of a man contrary to the testimony of his own consciousness. In all such cases, from the very laws of his being, he rejects all other testimony: and let me add, he would even reject the testimony of God, and from the very laws of his being must reject it, if it contradicted his own consciousness. When God convicts a man of sin, it is not by contradicting his consciousness. But God places the consciousness which he has at the time in the clear strong light of his memory, causing him to see clearly and to remember distinctly what light he had, what thoughts, and what convictions; in other words, what consciousness he had at the time. And this, let me add, is the way and the only way in which the Spirit of God can convict a man of sin, thus bringing him to condemn himself.

Now suppose that God should bear testimony against a man, that at such a time he did such a thing—that such and such were all the circumstances of the case—and suppose that, at the same time, the individual is unable to remember, and appears never to have had the least consciousness of the transaction. The testimony of God in this case could not satisfy the man's mind or lead him into a state of self-condemnation. The only possible way in which this state of mind could be induced would be to arouse the memory of past consciousness, and cause the whole scene to start into living reality before his mind's eye as it passed in his own consciousness at the time. But if he had no consciousness of any such thing, consequently no remembrance of it could possibly take place: to convict him of sin is naturally and forever impossible.

c. Men may overlook what consciousness is. They may mistake the rule of duty. They may confound consciousness with a mere negative state of mind, or with that state in which a man is not conscious of a state of opposition to the truth. Yet, it must forever remain true that to our own minds consciousness must be the highest possible evidence of what transpires within us. And if a man does not by his own consciousness know whether he does the best that he can, under the circumstances—whether he has a single eye to the glory of God—and whether he is in a state of entire consecration to God—he cannot know it in any way whatever. And no testimony whatever, either of God or man, could, according to the law of his being, satisfy him and produce in him either conviction of guilt on the one hand or self-approbation on the other.

Let me ask how those who make this objection know that *they* are *not* in a sanctified state? Has God *revealed* it to them? Has He revealed it in the Bible? Does the *Bible* say to particular individuals, by name, you are *not* in a sanctified state? Or does the Bible lay down a rule in the light of which his own consciousness bears this testimony against him? Has God revealed directly by His *Spirit* that he is not in a sanctified state? Or does He present the rule of duty strongly before the mind, and thus awaken the testimony of consciousness that he is not in this state?

Now in the same way, consciousness testifies to those who are sanctified that they *are* in that state. Neither the Bible nor the Spirit of God makes any new or particular revelation to them by name. But the Spirit of God bears witness with their spirits by setting the rule in a strong light before them. He brings about that state of mind that consciousness pronounces to be conformity to the rule. This does not set aside the judg-

ment of God in the case, for consciousness is, under these circumstances, the testimony of God and the way in which He
convinces of sin on the one hand and of entire consecration on
the other.

d. Some still object that consciousness alone is not evidence
even to ourselves of our being or not being in a state of entire
sanctification—that the judgment of the mind is also employed
in deciding the true intent and meaning of the law and is, therefore, as absolutely a witness in the case as consciousness is.
"Consciousness," some say, "gives us the exercises of our own
mind, and the judgment decides whether these exercises are in
accordance with the law of God." They argue that the judgment
rather than the consciousness decides whether we are or are
not in a state of entire sanctification. Therefore, if in our judgment of the law we happen to be mistaken, and nothing is more
common; in such a case we are utterly deceived, if we think
ourselves in a state of entire sanctification. I would concede that
it is indeed our judgment that decides on the intent and meaning of the law. And we may be mistaken in regard to its true
meaning and application in certain cases. But, I deny that it is
the judgment which is to us the witness in respect to the state
of our own minds. There are several powers of the mind called
into existence in deciding upon the meaning of, and obeying of,
the law of God; but it is consciousness alone that gives us these
exercises. Nothing but consciousness can possibly give us any
exercise of our own minds; that is, we have no knowledge of any
exercise but by our own consciousness. Suppose then the judgment, the will, and all the voluntary powers are exercised. These
exercises are revealed to us only and simply by consciousness;
so it remains an invariable truth that consciousness is to us the
only possible witness of what our exercises are, and consequently of the state of our own minds.

While I say that consciousness is the only evidence we have
or can have of our spiritual state, and of the exercises of our
own minds, it should be distinctly remembered that many
thoughts, emotions and affections go through our minds which
we do not so distinctly recognize at the time as to remember
them for an hour or perhaps for a moment. We must be indeed

slightly conscious of their existence at the time; but our minds being occupied so much with other things prevents us from giving attention to them so as to lodge them in our memories. Now of these thoughts, emotions and affections, which thus often pass through our minds in a great measure unnoticed, the following three things should be said, deeply pondered, well understood and always remembered: first, many of these thoughts, to say the least, must be sinful or holy. Second, if they are not distinctly noticed by consciousness, their moral character, whether sinful or holy, may at the time be overlooked by us. And third, as we have no distinct recollection of them, we may affirm that we are not *conscious* of sin, when as a matter of fact we may have been guilty of it in the exercise of these unnoticed thoughts and affections.

So, all that a man in this state of existence may ever be able to affirm in respect to his moral character is that he is not *conscious* of sin, without being able to say absolutely that he does not, and has not within a given time, had any exercise of mind that is sinful. When his mind is strongly exercised, and his consciousness therefore very clear and distinct, he may be able to affirm with a good degree of confidence, if not with certainty, that he has had no sinful exercises perhaps for a given time. But of the general tenor of his life, I do not see how he can affirm anything with more certainty than that he does not remember having been conscious of any sin.

This view of the subject will account for the fact to which I have already alluded: the way in which the Spirit of God always convinces of sin is by awakening in our memories the recollection of past consciousness, and often in this way revealing to us distinctly former states of mind of which we were but very slightly conscious at the time. The Holy Spirit makes us see that we have been guilty of committing sin of which we were not at all aware of before.

Paul seems to me to recognize this principle when he says, "But with me it is a very small thing that I should be judged of you, or of man's judgment: yea, I judge not mine own self. For I know nothing by myself; yet am I not hereby justified: but he that judgeth me is the Lord. Therefore judge nothing before the time, until the Lord come, who both will bring to light the hidden things of darkness, and will make manifest the counsels of the hearts: and then shall every man have praise of God" (1 Cor. 4:3–5). Here the Apostle says that he does not judge or try to decide fully respecting the perfection of his own character. "For I know nothing by myself; yet am I not hereby justified:" that is, if I understand him, "Though I am not conscious of any wrong, yet by this I am not justified." "But he that judgeth me is the Lord. Therefore judge nothing before the time, until the Lord come, who both will bring to light the hidden things of darkness, and make manifest the counsels of the hearts." By the "hidden things of darkness," in this context, the Apostle seems to me to refer to those states of mind of which at the time he had very slight consciousness, and were therefore immediately forgotten. Paul could not have meant that he formed no judgment whatever of his own character, or that he did not judge himself with respect to the general uprightness and holiness of his character, for this would make him contradict what he elsewhere affirms. He says that there might be things unperceived or unremembered about him of which he did not form a judgment, and could not therefore say that in no thought or affection he had been guilty of any wrong.

When, therefore, I say that by consciousness a man may know whether he is in a state of entire sanctification, I mean that consciousness is the real and only evidence that we can have of being in this state. When our minds are exercised strongly, and our consciousness therefore distinct, the testimony of consciousness is clear, explicit, and so satisfactory that we cannot doubt it. But under other circumstances and in other states of mind, when the exercises of the mind are such as to render consciousness less distinct and vivid, affections may be exercised by us, whether sinful or holy, that are not so distinctly noticed by consciousness, and so fully remembered by us that we can affirm absolutely that they were not sinful.

Again, the objection that consciousness cannot decide in regard to the strength of our powers, and whether we really serve God with *all* our strength, seems to be based on the false supposition that the law of God requires every power of body and mind to be excited at every moment to its full strength, and that too without any regard to the nature of the subject about which our powers for the time being are employed. Perfect obedience to the law of God requires no such thing. *Entire sanctification is entire consecration. Entire consecration is obedience to the law of God: and all that the law requires is that our whole being be consecrated to God, and the amount of strength to be expended in His service at any one moment of time must depend upon the nature of the subject about which the powers are for the time being exercised.* Nothing is further from the truth than that obedience to the law of God requires every power of body and mind to be constantly on the strain, and in the highest possible degree of excitement and activity. Such an interpretation of the law of God as this would be utterly inconsistent with life and health, and would write MENE, TEKEL, on the life and conduct of Jesus Christ himself; for His whole history shows that He was not in a state of constant excitement to the full extent of His powers.

2. Some object that if this state were attained in this life, it would be the end of our probation. To this I reply that probation since the fall of Adam, or those points in which we are in a state of probation or trial, are:

a. Whether we will repent and believe the gospel;

b. Whether we will persevere in holiness to the end of life.

Some assume the doctrine of the perseverance of the saints sets aside the idea of being in a state of probation after conversion. They reason thus: if it is certain that the saints will persevere, then their probation is ended; because the question is already settled, not only that they will be converted, but that they will persevere to the end, and the contingency in regard to the event is indispensable to the idea of probation. To this I reply:

A thing may be contingent with man that is not at all so with God. With God, there is not and never was any contingency with regard to the final destiny of any being. But with men, almost all things are contingencies. God knows with absolute certainty whether a man will be converted, and whether he will persevere. A man may know that he is converted, and may believe that by the grace of God he shall persevere. He may have an assurance of this in proportion to the strength of his faith. But the knowledge of this fact is not at all inconsistent with the idea of his continuance in a state of trial till the day of his death, in as much as his perseverance depends upon the exercise of his own voluntary agency.

In the same way some say that if we have attained a state of entire and permanent sanctification, we can no longer be in a state of probation. I answer that perseverance in this depends on the promises and grace of God, just as the final perseverance of the saints does. In neither case can we have any other assurance of our perseverance than that of faith in the promise and grace of God: nor any other knowledge that we shall continue in this state, than that which arises out of a belief in the testimony of God that He will preserve us blameless until the coming of our Lord Jesus Christ. If this is inconsistent with our probation, I do not see why the doctrine of the saint's perseverance is not equally inconsistent with it. If anyone is inclined to maintain that for us to have any judgment or belief in regard to our final perseverance is inconsistent with a state of probation, all I can say is that his views of probation are very different from my own, and so far as I understand, from those of the Church of God.

There is a very high and important sense in which every being will remain on probation throughout all eternity. While under the moral government of God, obedience must forever remain a condition of the favor of God. And the fact of continued obedience will forever depend on the faithfulness and grace of God; and the only knowledge we can ever have of this fact, either in heaven or on earth, must be founded on the faithfulness and truth of God.

If it were true that entering into a state of permanent sanctification in this life were in some sense an end of our probation, that would be no objection to the doctrine; for there is a sense in which probation often ends long before the termination of this life. Where, for example, a person has committed the unpardonable sin, or where from any cause God has given up sinners to fill up the measure of their iniquity, withdrawing forever His Holy Spirit from them and sealing them over to eternal death; this, in a very important sense, is the end of their probation and they are as sure of hell as if they were already there.

When a person has received the sealing of the Spirit unto the day of redemption as an earnest of his inheritance, he may and is bound to regard this as a solemn pledge on the part of God of his final perseverance and salvation, and as no longer leaving the final question of his destiny in doubt.

Now it should be remembered that in both these cases the result depends upon the exercise of the agency of the person. In the case of the sinner given up by God, it is certain that he will not repent, though his impenitence is voluntary and by no means a thing naturally necessary. So on the other hand, the perseverance of the saints is certain though not necessary. If in either case there should be a radical change of character, the result would differ accordingly.

3. While some admit that entire sanctification in this life is attainable, yet they deny that there is any certainty that it will be attained by anyone before death. For, they say, since all the promises of entire sanctification are conditioned upon faith, they *secure* the entire sanctification of no one. To this I reply:

All the promises of *salvation* in the Bible are conditioned on faith and repentance, and therefore it does not follow on this principle that any person ever will be saved. What does all this arguing prove? The fact is that while the promises of both salvation and sanctification are conditioned on faith as it respects individuals; yet to Christ and to the Church as a body, as I have already shown, these promises are unconditional. With respect to the salvation of sinners, it is promised that Christ shall have a seed to serve Him, and the Bible abounds with promises, both to Christ and the Church, that secure without condition, as it regards them, the salvation of great multitudes of sinners. So the promises that the Church as a body, at some period of her earthly history, shall be entirely sanctified, are, as it regards the Church, unconditional. But, as I have already shown, as it respects individuals, the fulfillment of these promises must depend upon the exercise of faith. Both in the salvation of sinners and the sanctification of Christians, God is abundantly pledged to bring about the salvation of the one and the sanctification of the other to the extent of His promise. But as it respects individuals, no one can claim the fulfillment of these promises without complying with the conditions.

These are the principal objections that have occurred to my mind, or that have so far as I know been emphasized by others. There may be, and doubtless are, others of greater or less plausibility to which I may have occasion to refer hereafter.

11

WHEN ENTIRE SANCTIFICATION IS ATTAINABLE

Having answered these objections to the doctrine of entire sanctification in this life, I will proceed *to show when entire sanctification is attainable.*

1. The blessing of entire sanctification is promised to Christians in both the Old and New Testaments, as shall be seen by the following verses.

Jeremiah 31:31–34: "Behold, the days come, saith the Lord, that I will make a new covenant with the house of Israel, and with the house of Judah: not according to the covenant that I made with their fathers in the day that I took them by the hand to bring them out of the land of Egypt; which my covenant they break, although I was an husband unto them, saith the Lord: but this shall be the covenant that I will make with the house of Israel; After those days, saith the Lord, I will put my law in their inward parts, and write it in their hearts; and will be their God, and they shall be my people. And they shall teach no more every man his neighbour, and every man his brother, saying, Know the Lord: for they shall all know me, from the least of them unto the greatest of them, saith the Lord: for I will forgive their iniquity, and I will remember their sin no more."

Ezekiel 36:25–27: "Then will I sprinkle clean water upon you, and ye shall be clean: from all your filthiness, and from all your idols, will I cleanse you. A new heart also will I give you, and a new spirit will I put within you: and I will take away the stony heart out of your flesh, and I will give you an heart of flesh. And I will put my spirit within you, and cause you to walk in my statutes, and ye shall keep my judgments and do them."

1 Thessalonians 5:23, 24: "And the very God of peace sanctify you wholly; and I pray God your whole spirit and soul and body be preserved blameless unto the coming of our Lord Jesus Christ. Faithful is he that calleth you, who also will do it."

Ephesians 1:13: "In whom ye also trusted, after that ye heard the word of truth, the gospel of your salvation: in whom also after that ye believed, ye were sealed with that holy Spirit of promise."

These and many others show that the promise is made to those who have some degree of faith, that is, who have been regenerated. The last verse says, we are sealed after we believe.

2. Faith is always the expressed or implied condition of the promises. It has been supposed that the promise in Jeremiah 31, together with other similar promises, is absolute in such a sense as to have no condition whatever. To this I reply that the things which they promise are of such a nature that they cannot possibly be received except by faith. Nor is faith the thing promised. The law of love cannot possibly be written in the heart, except through the faith which works by love. Therefore, this promise, of necessity, as well as all other promises of spiritual blessings, is conditioned on our faith.

It may be said that the promise to write the law in our hearts includes the doing of all that which is essential to its fulfillment; and therefore, a promise to beget love is virtually a promise to secure the right use of the means necessary to that end. But this excludes our own agency and responsibility. When Paul declared that not a hair of any man's head on board ship would perish, this did not exclude the necessity of the sailors remaining on board. For he afterward said, "except these abide in the ship, ye cannot be saved." Now it is true that in a very important sense, the promise that the hair of no man's head should perish implied that God would guarantee the use of the necessary means to save them. Yet who would infer from this that

that promise was not conditioned on the sailors remaining on board, and the right use of the voluntary agency of Paul and all the rest on board to save themselves. So it should be remembered that the promises to create a new heart and a new spirit—to make a new covenant with the house of Israel, and to write the law in their hearts—are certainly and necessarily conditioned upon the faith of everyone who would receive their fulfillment.

3. Regarding the doctrine of entire sanctification by faith, some have objected that faith is itself a holy exercise; therefore, faith is, for the time being, entire sanctification. They argue that to make faith the *condition* of entire sanctification is to make entire holiness the condition of entire holiness. To this I reply: sanctification is by faith in two senses.

a. Sanctification is by faith in opposition to sanctification by law, that is, the soul is sanctified by faith in Christ in opposition to legal sanctification. Christians are made holy by contemplating the love of Christ and by faith in Him and His Atonement instead of being made holy by the influence of legal considerations. This is evident from what the Apostle says in Romans 9:30–32: "What shall we say then? That the Gentiles, which followed not after righteousness, have attained to righteousness, even the righteousness which is of faith. But Israel, which followed after the law of righteousness, hath not attained to the law of righteousness. Wherefore? Because *they sought it* not by faith, but as it were by the works of the law. For they stumbled at that stumblingstone." The sanctification of the saints is effected only by renouncing all hope of justification or sanctification on the ground of law and by embracing Christ as our wisdom, righteousness, sanctification, and redemption. Faith is indeed a holy exercise; and therefore, is, in the lowest sense, entire sanctification. It is entire sanctification in the simple sense of a holy exercise.

b. It is not, however, a state of entire sanctification in the sense in which I use the term in this book, nor as I think in the sense in which the Bible uses the term. The sense in which I use the term entire sanctification includes all that is implied in perfect obedience to the law of God. In this sense of the term, it includes, if I may so speak, the whole family of holy exercises of which faith is one and only one. Entire sanctification includes all the modifications of benevolence, whereas faith is but one of the forms or modifications of holiness.

Who does not know that one holy exercise not only may be the condition of another, but that as a matter of fact faith is and must be the condition of the whole circle of holy affections?

4. This state is attainable on the ground of natural ability at any time. If this state were not attainable on the ground of natural ability, it would not be required and its absence would not be sin. But it has been doubted whether the work of entire sanctification is such, in its own nature, that it can be accomplished at once. To this I reply:

a. If it cannot be instantly accomplished, it would not be instantly required.

b. If it were not, in its own nature, capable of being attained at once, the non-attaining of it at once would not be sin. All that would be required would be to press forward as fast as we could.

c. But in this case the pressing forward would be a sinless state, because it would be all that could be required. So, we would possess at once, what according to the supposition is naturally impossible, that is, a state of entire sanctification.

d. I have already shown that provision is made against every temptation. If sufficient provision is made against all present and future temptation, since temptation, under some form is the cause of all sin, it follows that a state of entire sanctification is attainable at once.

5. *Full faith in the word and promise of God, naturally, certainly, and immediately produces a state of entire sanctification.* Understand that by faith I mean:

a. A realization of the truth and meaning of the Bible. And,

b. A laying hold upon all those truths upon which this state of mind depends, especially a full realization and belief of the sacred record God has given of His Son, that His blood "cleanseth us from all sin." It is easy to see that the realization and belief of the infinite love of God, as manifested in Christ Jesus, would have a tendency to fill the mind with unutterable and constant love to God—and produce the most cordial and perfect love to man. This result is instantaneous on the exercise of faith, and in this sense sanctification is an instantaneous work.

6. God is *able* to produce entire sanctification in any soul when He is pleased to do so.

This appears to be plainly taught by Christ, when He spoke of the ability of God to save the rich. He asserts that their salvation is more difficult than "for a camel to go through a needle's eye." And when the disciples expressed their astonishment, He replied that "the things which are impossible with men are possible with God" (Luke 18:25, 27). Now this seems to be a case in point. To *sanctify* the rich is the only difficulty in the way of their *salvation*. And Christ has asserted that God is able not only to sanctify them, but that "all things are possible with him"; that is, there is no limit to His ability in this respect.

Ephesians 3:20 proves the same point. Here the Apostle asserts that God is able to do "abundantly above all that we ask, and above all that we think," exceeding abundantly! Now we can both think of and ask for the blessing of entire, permanent, and instantaneous sanctification. According to this passage of Scripture, God is able to grant it.

God is able to produce present sanctification and also able to confirm us in a state of perpetual sanctification. The Scriptures say in Jude 24: "Now unto him that is able to keep you from falling, and to present you faultless before the presence of his glory with exceeding joy." Upon this passage I remark:

a. It asserts God is able to keep us from falling.

b. God is able to present us *faultless* before the presence of His glory.

c. Because God is able to keep us and to present us faultless, He is able to preserve us in a state of permanent sanctification. This verse declares He is able to do so.

To this it has been objected that moral government implies the power to resist every degree of motive. This I most fully admit. But it is one thing to have the power thus to resist, and quite another to use that power. God certainly knew when He created moral agents to what extent, and under what circumstances, they would actually exercise their power of resistance; and therefore, whether He could sanctify and save them or not. As a matter of fact, He has overcome the voluntary resistance of all who are converted. And if He has broken down their enmity, and so far subdued them, is it incredible that He should not be able wholly to sanctify them and preserve them blameless?

12

HOW ENTIRE SANCTIFICATION IS ATTAINED

In discussing sanctification, I now intend to *show how entire sanctification is attained.*

1. A state of entire sanctification can never be attained by an indifferent waiting for God's time.

2. A state of entire sanctification cannot be attained by any works of law, or works of any kind performed in your own strength irrespective of the grace of God. By this I do not mean that if you were disposed to exert your natural powers rightly, you could not at once obey the law in the exercise of your own strength. But I do mean that as you are wholly indisposed to use your natural powers rightly without the grace of God, no efforts that you will actually make in your own strength or independent of His grace will ever result in your entire sanctification.

3. We cannot attain it by any direct efforts to feel right. Many spend their time in vain efforts to force themselves into a right state of feeling. Now it should be forever understood that neither faith, love, repentance, nor any other right feeling is ever the result of a direct effort to put forth these feelings or exercises. But on the contrary, these right states of feeling are the spontaneous actings of the mind when it has under its direct and deep consideration *the objects* of faith, love and repentance. By spontaneous, I do not mean involuntary. They are the voluntary and the most easy and natural states of mind possible

under such circumstances. When the mind is intensely considering those objects and considerations, there is a natural tendency to produce right states of mind. This is so true that when persons are in the exercise of such affections, they feel no difficulty at all in their exercise, but wonder how anyone can help feeling as they do. It seems to them so natural, so easy, and I may say, so almost unavoidable, that they often feel and express astonishment that anyone should find it difficult to love, believe or repent.

The course that many persons take on the subject of religion has often appeared surprising to me. They make themselves, and their own state and interests, the central point around which their own minds are continually revolving. Their selfishness is so great that their own interests, happiness and salvation fill their whole field of vision. And with their thoughts, anxieties, and whole souls, clustering around their own salvation, they complain of a hard heart—that they cannot love God—that they do not repent and cannot believe. Being conscious that they do not feel right, they are the more concerned about themselves, which only increases their embarrassment and the difficulty of exercising right affections. The more deeply they feel, the more they try to feel—the greater efforts they make to feel right without success, the more they are confirmed in their selfishness. The more their thoughts are fixed on their own interests, the more they are at a greater and greater distance from any right state of feeling. And thus their selfish anxieties produce ineffective efforts, and these efforts only deepen their anxieties. If in this state, death should appear in a visible form before them, or the last trumpet sound and they should be summoned to the solemn Judgment, it would only increase their distraction, confirm and almost give omnipotence to their selfishness, and render their sanctification morally impossible.

4. Entire sanctification cannot be attained by any efforts to obtain grace by works of law. In my lecture on Faith, in the first volume of the *Evangelist*, I said the following things:*

---

*See *The Promise of the Spirit* for this lecture, published by Bethany House Publishers.

Should the question be proposed to a Jew, "What shall I do that I may work the works of God," he would answer, keep the law, both moral and ceremonial, that is, keep the commandments.

To the same inquiry an Arminian* would answer, improve common grace and you will obtain converting grace, that is, use the means of grace according to the best light you have, and you will obtain the grace of salvation. In this answer, it is not supposed that the inquirer already has faith and is using the means of grace in faith, but that he is in a state of impenitency and is inquiring after converting grace. The answer, therefore, amounts to this: you must get converting grace by your *impenitent* works; you must become holy by your hypocrisy; you must work out sanctification by sin.

To this question most professed Calvinists would make, in substance, the same reply. They would reject the language while they retained the idea. Their direction would imply either that the inquirer already has faith or that he must perform works to obtain it, that is, to obtain grace by works.

Neither an Arminian nor a Calvinist would *formally* direct the inquirer to the *law* as the ground of justification. But nearly the whole church would give directions that would amount to the same thing. Their answer would be a legal and not a gospel answer. For whatever answer is given to this question that does not distinctly recognize *faith* as the foundation of all virtue in sinners is legal. Unless the inquirer is made to understand that this is the first grand fundamental duty, without the performance of which all virtue, all giving up of sin, all acceptable obedience is impossible, he is misdirected. He is led to believe that it is possible to please God without faith and to obtain grace by works of law. There are but two kinds of works, works of law and works of faith. Now if the inquirer has not the "faith that works by love," to set him upon any course of works to get it is certainly to direct him to get faith by works of law. What-

---

*Finney here uses the word "Arminian" in the sense usual among nineteenth-century Christians of Calvinist background, as a synonymn for "Pelagian," that is, one who affirms salvation by good works. Methodists, understandably, deplored this usage.

ever is said to him that does not clearly convey the truth that both justification and sanctification are by faith, without works of law, is law and not gospel. Nothing before or without faith can possibly be done by the unbeliever but works of law. His first duty, therefore, is faith; and every attempt to obtain faith by unbelieving works is to lay works at the foundation and make grace a result. It is the direct opposite of gospel truth.

Take facts as they arise in every day's history to show that what I have stated is the experience of almost all, professors and nonprofessors. Whenever a sinner begins in good earnest to agitate the question, "what shall I do to be saved," he resolves as a first duty to break off from his sins, that is, in unbelief. Of course his reformation is only outward; he determines to do better, to reform in this, that and the other thing, and thus prepare himself to be converted. He does not expect to be saved without grace and faith but he attempts to get grace by works of law.

The same is true of multitudes of anxious Christians who are inquiring what they shall do to overcome the world, the flesh and the devil. They overlook the fact that "this is the victory that overcometh the world, even your faith," that it is with "the shield of faith" that they are "to quench all the fiery darts of the wicked." They ask, why am I overcome by sin? Why can I not get above its power? Why am I thus the slave of my appetites and passions and the sport of the devil? They cast about for the cause of all this spiritual wretchedness and death. At one time they think they have discovered it in the neglect of one duty, and at another time in the neglect of another. Sometimes they imagine they have found the cause to lie in yielding to one sin and sometimes in yielding to another. They put forth efforts in this direction and in that direction and patch up their righteousness on one side while they make a rent in the other. Thus they spend years in running around in a circle and making dams of sand across the current of their own corruptions. Instead of at once *purifying their hearts by faith*, they are engaged in trying to arrest the overflowing of its bitter waters. *Why* do I sin, they inquire; and casting about for the cause they come to the sage conclusion, it is because I neglect such a duty, that is, because I do sin. But how shall I get rid of sin? Answer: by doing my duty, that is, by ceasing from sin. Now the real inquiry is, *why* do they neglect their duty? Why do they commit sin at all? Where is the foundation of all this mischief? Will it be replied, the foundation of all this wickedness is in the corruption of our nature, in the wickedness of the heart, in the strength of our evil propensities and habits? But all this only brings us back to the real inquiry again: how are this corrupt nature, this wickedness and these sinful habits to be overcome? I answer, by faith alone. No works of law have the least tendency to overcome our sins but rather confirm the soul in self-righteousness and unbelief.

The great and fundamental sin which is at the foundation of all other sin is unbelief. The first thing is to give up that—to believe the Word of God. There is no breaking off from one sin without this. "Whatever is not of faith is sin." "Without faith it is impossible to please God." Thus we see that the backslider and convicted Christian, when agonizing to overcome sin, will almost always betake themselves to works of law to obtain faith. They will fast and pray and read and struggle and outwardly reform, and thus endeavor to obtain grace. Now all this is in vain and wrong. Do you ask, shall we not fast and pray and read and struggle? Shall we do nothing but sit down in Antinomian security and inaction? I answer, you must do all that God commands you to do; but begin where He tells you to begin and do it in the manner in which He commands you to do it, that is, in the exercise of that faith that works by love. Purify your hearts by faith. Believe in the Son of God. And say not in your heart, "Who shall ascend into heaven?" (that is, to bring Christ down from above); or "Who shall descend into the deep?" (that is to bring up Christ again from the dead), "But what saith it? The word is nigh thee, even in thy mouth, and in thy heart: that is, the word of faith, which we preach."

Now these facts show that even under the gospel almost all professors of religion, while they reject the Jewish notion of justification by works of the law, have after all adopted a ruinous substitute for it and suppose that in some way they are to obtain grace by their works.

5. A state of entire sanctification cannot be attained by attempting to copy the experience of others. It is very common for convicted sinners in their blindness, or for Christians inquiring after entire sanctification, to ask others to relate their experience, to carefully note the detail of all their exercises, and then set themselves to pray for and make direct efforts to attain the same class of exercises. They do not seem to understand that they can no more exercise feelings in detail like others than they can look like others.

Human experiences differ as human countenances differ. The whole history of a man's former state of mind comes in to modify his present and future exercises. The precise sequence of affections which may be requisite in your case, and which will actually occur in your case, if you are ever sanctified, will not in all its detail coincide with the exercises of any other human being. It is extremely important for you to understand that you cannot copy exactly any true religious experience; and that you are in a great danger of being deceived by Satan whenever you attempt to copy the experience of others. I beseech you, therefore, to cease from praying for or trying to obtain the precise experience of any other person. All truly Christian experiences are, like human countenances in their outline, so much alike as to be readily known as the characteristics of the religion of Jesus Christ. But no further than this are they alike, any more than human countenances are alike.

6. This state cannot be attained by waiting to make preparations before you enter in. Observe that the thing about which you are inquiring is a state of entire consecration to God. Now do not imagine that this state of mind must be prefaced by a long introduction of preparatory exercises. It is common for persons, when inquiring upon this subject with earnestness, to think themselves hindered in their progress by a lack of this or that, or the other exercise or state of mind. They look everywhere else but at the real difficulty. They find many reasons but the true reason for their not being already in a state of sanctification.

7. A state of entire sanctification cannot be attained by attending meetings, asking the prayers of other Christians, or

depending in any way upon the means of getting into this state. By this I do not intend to say that means are unnecessary, or that it is not through the instrumentality of truth that this state of mind is induced. But I do mean that while you are depending on any instrumentality whatever, your mind is diverted from the real point at hand and you are not likely to make this attainment.

8. Entire sanctification will not be attained by waiting for any particular views of Christ. When persons, in the state of mind of which I have been speaking, hear those who live in faith describe their views of Christ, they say, "Oh, if I had such *views*, I could believe; I must have these before I can believe." Now you should understand that these *views* are the result and effect of faith. These views of which you speak are those which faith discovers in those passages of Scripture which describe Christ. Faith apprehends the meaning of those passages, and sees in them those very things which you expect to see before you exercise faith, and which you imagine would produce it.* Take hold, then, of the simple promise of God. Take God at His Word. Believe He means just what He says; and this will immediately bring you into the state of mind which you are seeking.

9. Entire sanctification will not be attained in any way which you may mark out for yourself. Persons in an inquiring state are very apt, without seeming to be aware of it, to send imagination on before them. They stake out the way and set up a flag where they intend to come out. They expect to be thus and thus exercised—to have certain peculiar views and feelings, when they have attained their goal. Now there probably never was a person who did not find himself disappointed in these respects. God says, "I will bring the blind by a way that they knew not; I will lead them in paths that they have not known: I will make darkness light before them, and crooked things straight. These things will I do unto them, and not forsake them" (Isa. 42:16).

---

*See especially *Principles of Union with Christ*, published by Bethany House Publishers.

Allowing your imagination to mark out your path is a great hindrance to you. It sets you on many fruitless, and worse than fruitless, attempts to attain this imaginary state of mind. It wastes much of your time. It greatly wearies the patience and grieves the Spirit of God. While He is trying to lead you right to the point, you are veering from the course and insisting that your imagination has marked out the way. You ignore the way in which He is trying to lead you. And thus in your pride and ignorance you are causing much delay and abusing the long suffering of God. He says, "This is the way, walk ye in it." But you say, "No—this is the way." And thus you stand and talk and joke while you are every moment in danger of grieving the Spirit of God away from you, and of losing your soul.

10. Sanctification is not attainable in any manner or at any time or place on which you may in your own mind place any emphasis. If there is anything in your imagination that has definitely fixed upon any particular manner, time, place or circumstance, you will in all probability either be deceived by the devil or entirely disappointed in the result. You will find that all these particular items which you have emphasized in the wisdom of man is foolishness with God. You will discover your ways are not His ways, nor your thoughts His thoughts. "For as the heavens are higher than the earth, so are my ways higher than your ways, and my thoughts than your thoughts" (Isa. 55:9).

11. Entire sanctification is to be attained by faith alone. Let it be forever remembered, "without faith it is impossible to please God," and "whatsoever is not of faith is sin."

Both justification and sanctification are by faith alone. Scripture teaches, in Romans 3:30: "Seeing it is one God, which shall justify the circumcision by faith, and uncircumcision through faith"; and Romans 5:1: "Therefore being justified by faith, we have peace with God through our Lord Jesus Christ." Also, Romans 9:30, 31: "What shall we say then? That the Gentiles, which followed not after righteousness, have attained to righteousness, even the righteousness which is of faith. But Israel, which followed after the law of righteousness, hath not attained to the law of righteousness. Wherefore? Because they sought it not by faith, but as it were by the works of the law."

So you may clearly understand this part of the subject, I will quote again from my lecture in the first volume of the *Evangelist*, the elements that constitute saving faith.

a. The first element of saving faith is a realizing sense of the truth of the Bible. This alone is not saving faith, for Satan has this realizing sense of truth which makes him tremble.

b. A second element in saving faith is the consent of the heart or will to the truth perceived by the intellect. It is cordial trust or resting of the mind in those truths, yielding up of the whole being to their influence. Now it is easy to see that without the confidence of the heart, there can be nothing but an outward obedience to God. Without confidence in her husband, a wife can do nothing more than perform her duty outwardly to him. It is a contradiction to say that without confidence she can perform her duty from the heart. The same is true of parental and all other governments. Works of law may be performed without faith; that is, we may serve from fear or hope, or some selfish consideration, but without the confidence that works by love, obedience from the heart is naturally impossible. Obedience from the heart without love is a contradiction.

c. Faith is the most simple and rational state of mind conceivable. Faith is that state of mind for which very young children are so remarkable. Before they have been taught distrust by the hypocrisy and depravity of others, they seem to know nothing of unbelief. They are so simple and honest that they feel entire confidence in those around them. Faith is merely a trust in testimony, a resting of the heart in truths perceived by the intellect, a natural yielding of the voluntary powers to the testimony of God.

d. Faith is a spontaneous state of mind. It is not, as I have said, the result of an effort to believe. Faith is the natural resting or reposing of the mind in the truth of God. When the soul believes, all that it can say is, "while I mused the fire burned," when I thought on the truth to be believed, before I was aware, I found myself believing. As I have already said, I do not mean this is an involuntary state of mind. Faith is voluntary in so high a sense as not to be the result of effort. Faith is the joyful, natural and easy yeilding up of the mind to the influence of truth.

e. Faith discovers the real meaning and apprehends the fullness of those passages that describe Christ. Faith presents Christ to the mind not as one at a distance, but as one who is near, not as enveloped in clouds, but (in those passages that describe Him) as beheld in a fullness and a glory and surpassing loveliness that overpowers and melts the soul.

f. The truths to be believed, in order to induce this state of mind, are those which comprise "the record that God has given of His Son." The mind needs to apprehend God in Christ. To be like God, we must know what He is. To be led to a spontaneous consecration of all to Him, our selfishness must be overcome by a knowledge of what God is. And this knowledge is to be obtained only by seeing God in Christ. For this very purpose God took upon himself human nature, that He might reveal himself to the sons of men, and thus present to their minds a true knowledge of His character.

g. The natural and certain effect of knowing God is a state of entire consecration to Him. I have said that while individuals are taken up with contemplating themselves, (their own characters, dangers, and troubles) they cannot be sanctified. There is no tendency in such considerations to produce a state of sanctification. They may dwell on their own misery or wretchedness throughout all eternity without finding it possible to consecrate themselves to God. What is there in such considerations that can in any way produce such a result? The consideration of the infinite excellence of Christ's character, and this alone, can inspire faith or love. If, therefore, you ever expect to trust in God, and love Him with all your heart, you must acquaint yourself with the reasons for thus loving and trusting Him. You must know God. You must have the true knowledge of God. God, and not yourselves, must be the object of your thoughts.

Cease then, I beseech you, to expect to be sanctified by any works of your own, or any direct efforts to feel or to do more or less, and remember "That faith cometh by hearing." Understand and believe the record that God has given of His Son and at once you will be given an experimental acquaintance with the truth that "the blood of Jesus Christ his Son cleanseth us from all sin."

12. The New and the Old dispensations differ in two respects.

a. The New is a fuller and more perfect revelation of Christ, or of those things that are indispensable to sanctification.

b. There is a much greater amount of the Holy Spirit's influence exerted under this dispensation. The Old made nothing perfect, because of the obscure nature of the revelation of Christ, and because there was not a sufficient degree of divine influence to fully possess the mind of the truths indispensable to permanent sanctification. The mind must know enough of God to slay selfishness, and without this neither love nor permanent sanctification is possible. Blessed be God! With the influences of the Holy Spirit, the New dispensation has brought us into the clear sunlight and revealed God so as to overcome sin.

13. In conclusion I would remark:

It is useless to speculate on any supposed distinction that might have been in the Apostle's mind between the soul and spirit of man, when he penned the passage which stands at the beginning of this book. I understand the prayer of the Apostle to be for the entire consecration of the whole being to the service of God. I need not dwell any more on the text, except to mention some things which I suppose are implied in the entire sanctification of the body.

a. I understand the sanctification of the body to imply the entire consecration of the body by the soul, of all its members to the service of God. The body is to be regarded merely as the instrument of the soul through which it manifests itself and by which it fulfills its desires.

b. The entire sanctification of the body also implies the entire consecration of all its appetites and passions to the service of God. All its appetites will only be used for the purposes for which they were designed, not to be the masters, but the servants of the soul, not to lead the soul away from God, but to subserve the highest interests of the physical organization.

c. It implies controlling the body, and bringing it into subjection, so that no appetite or passion of the body is indulged merely for the sake of the indulgence. No appetite or passion is to be consulted at any time, or its indulgence allowed but for the glory of God, to answer the end of our being, and to render us useful in the highest degree.

The grand error of mankind is that the soul has been debased so as to be the slave of the body. The appetites and passions have ruled. The "fleshly mind which is enmity against God," has been allowed to become the law of the soul. Hence, the Apostle complains that he saw "a law in his members, warring against the law of his mind, bringing him into captivity to the law of sin and death," which was in his members. He writes, "if ye live after the flesh, ye shall die," and "they that are after the flesh do mind the things of the flesh," that, "to be carnally minded is death," that "he that soweth to his flesh shall of the flesh reap corruption." In short, throughout the Bible it is expressly taught that one great error and sin of mankind is the indulgence of the flesh.

d. Now the entire sanctification of the body implies the denial of the lusts of the flesh, that we put "on the Lord Jesus Christ, and make no provision for the flesh, to fulfill the lusts thereof." The appetites and passions must be restrained and entirely subjugated to the highest interest and perfection of the soul and to the glory of God. The highest sense in which the body may be sanctified in this life implies the strictest temperance in all things. By temperance I mean the moderate use of things that are useful, and total abstinence from things that are detrimental.

It implies also the utter denial of all the artificial appetites of the body. By artificial appetites I mean all those appetites that are not natural to man previous to all depravity of the system by any kind of abuse or violation of its laws. Among the artificial appetites are all those hankerings after various poisons, narcotics, and non-nutritious stimulants that are in almost universal use; including, in my opinion, tobacco, tea, coffee, and the like. The use of all such substances is utterly inconsistent with perfect temperance, worse than useless, and produces only a temporary excitement at the expense of certain and permanent debility. They deceive mankind on the same principle that alcohol has so long deceived men, and though not to the same degree injurious and inconsistent with the highest well-being of the body and soul, yet they are as really so and therefore utterly unlawful. Only ignorance can prevent their use from being sin; and when the means of knowledge are at hand, this ignorance itself becomes sin. Consequently, persevering in this use under such circumstances is not only inconsistent with entire and permanent sanctification, but also with justification and salvation.

Temperance implies a knowledge of and compliance with all the laws of our physical system. There is scarcely any branch of knowledge more important to mankind than a knowledge of the structure and laws of our own being. Nor is there scarcely any subject on which men are so generally and so shamefully ignorant. It seems mankind in general does not know or even suspect that everything about their bodies is regulated by laws. A perfect knowledge of and conformity to these laws would render permanent health as certain as the law of gravitation renders the regular motion of the planets. The world is full of disease and premature death, and men speak of these things as mysterious providences of God without ever so much as dreaming that they are the natural and certain results of the most outrageous and reckless violations of the laws of the human body.

Temperance in all things implies correct diet and other habits regarding exercise and rest. In short, such obedience in all respects to the physiological laws of the body so as to promote its highest degree of physical perfection, and thus preserve it in a state in which it will be in the highest degree capable of being used by the soul, is to fulfill the will of God. There are, no doubt, occasions on which the bodily strength and the body itself may be sacrificed to the interests of the soul, and of the Redeemer's kingdom—cases in which the violation of physical law may be justifiable and even a duty, where the kingdom of Christ demands the sacrifice. Christ gave up His body as a sacrifice. The Apostles and martyrs gave up theirs. And in every age multitudes have given themselves up to such labors for the kingdom of Christ that have soon ended their mortal lives. This is not inconsistent with the highest consecration of the body and of the whole being to God. On the other hand, it is one of the highest instances of such consecration. But where the circumstances do not demand it, the sanctification of the body implies that its strength shall not be exhausted, nor any of its powers debilitated or injured by any neglect of exercise, or by any overworking of its organs, or by any vindication of its laws whatever. It implies the utmost regularity in all our habits of eating, drinking, sleeping, labor, rest, exercise, and in short, a strictly religious regard to all those things that can contribute to our highest perfection of body and soul.

Can a glutton, who is stupified two or three times a day with his food, be entirely consecrated either in body or soul to God? Certainly not. His table is a snare, and a trap, and a stumbling block to him. Can an epicure, whose tastes loathe every correctly prepared article of diet, and who demands that every meal should be prepared with seasonings and condiments highly injurious to the health of his body and the well-being of his soul—can he be in a state of entire consecration to God? No! Surely, his "god is his belly." His "glory is in his shame." He "minds earthly things." And an Apostle would tell him, "even weeping, that his end is destruction."

It is appalling to see the various forms of disease and wretchedness with which mankind are cursed on account of their wanton disregard of the laws of their being. The highest powers of the human mind can never be developed, nor its highest perfection attained, in a diseased body. Probably scarcely a single member of the human family in his present state has anything like perfect health. Many suppose themselves to be perfectly healthy, simply because they never saw a person who had perfect health, and also because they do not know enough of themselves to know that many of their organs may be fatally diseased without their being aware of it.

The influence of dietetic and other habits on the health of the body is known to but a very limited extent among mankind; and far less is it understood that whatever affects the body inevitably affects the mind. The temper and spirit of a man are in a great measure modified by the state of his health. It is known to some extent that an acid stomach produces fretfulness, and that certain nervous diseases, as they are called, greatly affect the mind. But it is not so generally known as it ought to be that all our dietetic and other physiological habits have a powerful influence in forming and molding our moral character. Not necessarily or absolutely, but by way of temptation, they act through our bodily organs. All stimulants and all things injurious to the body act very detrimentally on the mind. If you expect the sanctification of body, soul and spirit, you must acquaint yourselves with the true principles of temperance and physiological reform, and must discipline yourself to conform yourselves to them not only in the aggregate but in the detail.

13

CONCLUSION

1. Very few persons appear to be aware of the importance to be attached to the sanctification of the body. Indeed, unless the bodily appetites and powers are consecrated to the service of God, unless we learn to eat and drink and sleep and wake and labor and rest for the glory of God, entire and permanent sanctification is out of the question.

a. Very few persons are aware of the great influence which their bodies have over their minds, and of the indispensable necessity of bringing their bodies under control and keeping them in subjection.

Few people seem to constantly remember that unless their bodies are rightly managed, they will be so fierce and overpowering a source of temptation to the mind, as inevitably to lead it into sin. If they indulge themselves in a stimulating diet, and in the use of those condiments that irritate and rasp the nervous system, their bodies will be, of necessity, the source of powerful and incessant temptation to evil tempers and vile affections. If persons were aware of the great influence which the body has over the mind, they would realize that they cannot be too careful to preserve the nervous system from the influence of every improper article of food or drink, and preserve that system as they would the apple of their eye from every influence that could impair its functions.

b. No one, who has opportunity to acquire information in regard to the laws of life and health and the best means of sanctifying the whole spirit, soul, and body, can be guiltless if he neglects these means of knowledge. Everyone is bound to make the structure and laws of both body and mind the subject of as thorough an investigation as his circumstances will permit. He must be informed with regard to what are the true principles of perfect temperance, and in what way the most can be made of all his powers of body and mind for the glory of God.

2. From what has been said in this book, the reason why the Church has not been entirely sanctified is very obvious. As a body, the Church has not believed that such a state was attainable in this life. And this is a sufficient reason, and indeed the best of all reasons, for her not having attained it.

a. From what has been said, it is easy to see that the true question in regard to entire sanctification in this life is, Is it attainable as a matter of fact? Some have thought the proper question to be, Are Christians entirely sanctified in this life? Suppose it were fully granted that they are not; this fact is sufficiently accounted for by the consideration that they do not know or believe it to be attainable in this life. If they believed it to be attainable, it might no longer be true that they do not attain it. But if provision really is made for this attainment, it amounts to nothing unless it is recognized and believed. The thing needed then is to bring the Church to see and believe that this is her high privilege and her duty.

b. It is not enough to say that it is attainable, simply on the ground of natural ability. This is as true of the devil, and of the lost in hell, as of men in this world. But unless grace has put this attainment so within our reach, so that it may be aimed at with the reasonable prospect of success, there is, as a matter of fact, no more provisions for our entire sanctification in this life than for the devil's.

It seems to be trifling with mankind merely to maintain the attainability of this state on the ground of natural ability only. The real question is, Has grace brought this attainment so within reach that we may reasonably expect to experience it in this life? It is admitted that on the ground of natural ability both wicked men and devils have the power to be entirely holy. But it is also admitted that their indisposition to use this power rightly is so complete, that as a matter of fact, they never will unless influenced to do so by the grace of God. I insist, therefore, that the real question is, Are the provisions of the gospel such, that, if the Church did fully understand and lay hold of the offered grace, would she as a matter of fact attain this state?

We see how irrelevant and absurd the objection is that, as a matter of fact, the Church has not attained this state; therefore, it is not attainable. Why, if they have not understood it to be attainable, it no more proves its unattainableness than the fact that the heathen have not embraced the gospel proves that they will not when they know it.

3. You see the necessity of fully preaching and insisting on this doctrine and of calling it by its true Scriptural name. It is astonishing to see to what an extent there is a tendency among men to avoid the use of Scriptural language, and cleave to the language of such men as Edwards and other great and good theologians. They object to the terms perfection and entire sanctification, and prefer to use the terms entire consecration, and other such terms as have been common in the Church.

Now, I would by no means contend about the use of words; but it still appears to me to be very important that we use Scriptural language and insist on men being "*perfect* as their Father in Heaven is perfect," and being "*sanctified* wholly, body, soul, and spirit." It is very important to use Scriptural terms because if we use the language to which the Church has been accustomed on this subject, she will, as she has done, misunderstand us, and will not really understand what we really mean. This is obvious from the fact that the great mass of the Church will express alarm at the use of the terms perfection and entire sanctification, but they will neither express nor feel any such alarm if we speak of entire consecration. This demonstrates that they do not, by any means, understand these terms to mean the same thing. And although I understand them as meaning precisely the same thing, yet I find myself obliged to use the terms perfection and entire sanctification to convince their minds of my real meaning. This is Bible language. It is unobjectionable language. And inasmuch as the Church understands entire consecration to mean something less than entire sanctification or Christian perfection, it seems very important to me that ministers use phraseology which will call the attention of the Church to the real doctrine of the Bible on this subject. And I would submit the question with great humility to my beloved brethren in the ministry: Are they not aware that Christians have entirely too low an idea of what is implied in entire consecration, and is it not useful and best to adopt a phraseology in addressing them that will call their attention to the real meaning of the words which they use?

4. Young converts have not been allowed so much as to indulge the thought that they could live even for a day wholly without sin. As a general thing, they have no more been taught to expect to live even for a day without sin, than they have been taught to expect immediate translation, soul and body, to heaven. They have not known that there was any other way but to continue in sin. However shocking and distressing the necessity of continual sinning has appeared to them in the ardor of their first love, still they have looked upon it as an unalterable fact that to be in a great measure in bondage to sin is an inevitable thing while they live in this world. Now with such an orthodoxy as this, so prevalent throughout the Church and ministry (that the utmost the grace of God can do for men in this world is to bring them to repentance and to leave them to live and die in a state of sinning and repenting), is it at all surprising that the state of religion should be as it really has been?

In looking over the results of preaching the doctrine of entire sanctification to Christians, I feel compelled to say that, in all my observations, I have the same evidence that this doctrine is true, and as such is owned and blessed of God to the sanctification of Christians, as I have that those are truths which I have so often preached to sinners, and which have been so often and so eminently blessed of God to their conversion. This doctrine seems as naturally calculated to elevate the piety of Christians, and as actually to result in the elevation of their piety under the blessing of God as those truths that I preached to sinners were to their conversions.

5. Christ has been, in a great measure, lost sight of in some

of His most important relations to mankind. He has been known and preached as a pardoning and justifying Savior, but as an actually indwelling and reigning Savior in the heart, He has been very little known.*

I was impressed with the remark, a few years ago, made by a brother whom I have from that time greatly loved. He had been in a despondent state of mind for a time, burdened with a great sense of his own vileness, and seeing no way of escape. At an evening meeting, the Lord so revealed himself to him that the strength of his body was entirely overcome, and his brethren were obliged to carry him home. The next time I saw him he exclaimed to me with a pathos I shall never forget, "Brother Finney, the Church has buried the Savior." Now it is no doubt true that the Church has become awfully alienated from Christ. She has, in a great measure, lost a knowledge of what He is and ought to be to her. And a great many of her members, I have good reason to know, in different parts of the country, are saying with deep and overpowering emotion, "They have taken away my Lord and I know not where they have laid Him."

With all her orthodoxy, the Church has been for a long time much nearer to Unitarianism than she has imagined. This remark may shock some of my readers, and you may think it savors of censoriousness. But, beloved, I am sure it is said in no such spirit. These are "the words of truth and soberness." So little has been known of Christ, that, if I am not entirely mistaken, there are multitudes in the orthodox churches who do not know Christ and who in heart are Unitarians, while in theory they are orthodox.

I have been deeply impressed with the fact that so many professors of religion are coming to the ripe conviction that they never knew Christ. I doubt whether there is a minister in the land who will present Christ as the gospel presents Him, in all the fullness of His official relations to mankind, who will not be struck and agonized with developments that will assure him

---

*See especially, *Principles of Union with Christ*, published by Bethany House Publishers.

that the great mass of those who profess to be religious do not know the Savior.

What I ought to think of the spiritual state of those who know so little of the blessed Jesus has been to my own mind a painful and serious question. That none of them have been converted, I dare not say. And yet, that they have been converted, I am *afraid* to say. I would not for the world "quench the smoking flax or break the bruised reed," or say anything to stumble or weaken the feeblest lamb of Christ; and yet my heart aches. My soul is sick; my bowels of compassion yearn over the Church of the blessed God. Oh, the dear Church of Christ! What does she in her present state know of gospel rest, of that "great and perfect peace which they have whose minds are stayed in God?"

6. If I am not mistaken, there is an extensive feeling among Christians and ministers that there is a great lack of what ought to be made known and may be known of the Savior. Many are beginning to find that the Savior is to them "as a root out of dry ground, having neither form nor comeliness." The gospel which they preach and hear is not to them "the power of God unto salvation" *from sin*. It is not "glad tidings of great joy," nor is it a peace-giving gospel. Many are feeling that if Christ has done all that His grace is able to do in this life for them, then the plan of salvation is sadly defective, and Christ is not a Savior suited to their necessities after all. The religion which they have is not suited to the world in which they live; it does not, cannot make them free, but leaves them in a state of perpetual bondage. Their souls are agonized and tossed to and fro without a resting place. Multitudes also are beginning to see that there are many passages, both in the Old and New Testaments, which they do not understand; that the promises seem to mean much more than they have ever realized, and that the gospel and the plan of salvation as a whole must be something very different from that which they have as yet apprehended. There are great multitudes all over the country who are inquiring more earnestly than ever before after a knowledge of that Jesus who is to save His people from their sins.

A fact was related to me that illustrates in a moving way the agonizing state of mind in which many Christians are in with regard to the present state of many of the ministers of Christ. I heard the statement from the brother himself, who was the subject of his narrative. A sister in the church where he preached was keenly aware that he did not know Christ as he ought to know Him, and because of that she was full of unutterable agony. On one occasion, after he had been preaching, she fell down at his feet crying and strongly imploring him to exercise faith in Christ. At another time she was so impressed with a sense of his deficiency in this respect, as a minister, that she addressed him in the deepest anguish of her soul, crying out: "Oh, I shall die, I shall certainly die, unless you will receive Christ as a full Savior." And attempting to approach him, she sank down helpless, overcome with agony and travail of soul at his feet.

There is manifestly a great struggle in the minds of multitudes, that the Savior may be more fully revealed to the Church, that the present ministry especially may know Him, the power of His resurrection, the fellowship of His sufferings, and be made conformable to His death.

7. If the doctrine of entire sanctification is true, you see the immense importance of preaching it clearly and fully in revivals of religion. When the hearts of converts are warm with their first love, then is the time to make them fully acquainted with their Savior, to hold Him up in all His offices and relations, so as to break the power of every sin—to break them off forever from all self-dependence and to lead them to receive Christ as a present, perfect, everlasting Savior.*

Unless this course is taken, their backsliding is inevitable. You might as well expect to roll back the waters of Niagara with your hand, as to stay the time of their corruption without a deep and thorough and experimental acquaintance with the Savior. And if they are thrown upon their own watchfulness and resources for strength against temptation, instead of being directed to the Savior, they are certain to become discouraged and fall into continual bondage.

---

*See Finney's *Principles of Union with Christ*, published by Bethany House Publishers, for his exposition of the relationship Jesus Christ wants to have with each person according to His titles in the Scriptures.

8. But before I conclude these remarks, I must point out the indispensable necessity of a *willingness* to do the will of God in order to rightly understand this doctrine. If a man is unwilling to give up his sins, to deny himself all ungodliness and every worldly lust—if he is unwilling to be set apart wholly to the service of the Lord, he will either reject this doctrine altogether or only intellectually admit it without receiving it into his heart. It is an imminently dangerous state of mind to assent to this or any doctrine of the gospel and not reduce it to practice.

Much evil has been done by those who have professedly embraced this doctrine in theory and rejected it in practice. Their spirit and temper have been such as to lead those who saw them to infer that the tendency of the doctrine itself is bad. And it is not to be doubted that *some* who have professed to have experienced the power of this doctrine in their hearts have greatly disgraced religion by exhibiting any other spirit than that of an entirely sanctified person. But why, in a Christian land, should this be a stumblingblock? When the *heathen* see persons from Christian nations, who professedly adopt the Christian system, exhibit on their shores and in their countries the spirit which many of them do, they infer that this is the tendency of the Christian religion. To this our missionaries reply that they are only nominal Christians, only speculative and not real believers. If thousands of our *church members* were to go among them, they would have the same reason to complain and might reply to the missionaries, "These are not only nominal believers, but they profess to have experienced the Christian religion in their own hearts." Now what would the missionaries reply? Why, to be sure, that they were professors of religion, but that they really did not know Christ, that they were deceiving themselves, thinking themselves to be alive, while in fact they were dead in trespasses and sins.

I have often been astonished that in a Christian land it should be a stumblingblock to anyone, that there are many who profess to receive and to have experienced the truth of this doctrine, and yet exhibit an unchristian spirit. What if the same objection should be brought against the Christian religion, against any and every doctrine of the gospel, that the great majority, and even nine tenths of all the professed believers and receivers of those doctrines were proud, worldly, selfish, and exhibited anything but a right spirit? Now this objection might be made with truth to the professedly Christian Church. But would the conclusiveness of such objections be admitted in Christian lands? The doctrines of Christianity do not sanction such conduct, for anyone who displays such a spirit or conduct holds not the true belief in his heart for the Christian religion abhors all these objectionable things.

Now suppose it should be replied that a tree is known by its fruits, and that so great a majority of the professors of religion could not exhibit such a spirit, unless it were the tendency of Christianity itself to produce it. Now who would not reply to this saying this state of mind and course of conduct of which they complain is the natural state of man uninfluenced by the gospel of Christ; that in these instances, on account of unbelief, the gospel has failed to correct what was already wrong, and that it did not need the influence of any corrupt doctrine to produce that state of mind? It appears to me that those who object to this doctrine, on account of the fact that some and perhaps many who have professed to receive it have exhibited a wrong spirit, take it for granted that the doctrine *produces* this spirit instead of considering that a wrong spirit is natural to men, and that the difficulty is that through unbelief the gospel has failed to correct what was wrong before. They reason as if they supposed the human heart needed something to produce a bad spirit within it, and as if they supposed a belief in this doctrine had made men wicked, instead of recognizing the fact they were wicked before, and through unbelief the gospel has failed to make them holy.

Let it not be understood that I suppose or admit that any considerable number who have professed to have received this doctrine into their hearts have, as a matter of fact, exhibited a bad spirit. I must say that it has been eminently otherwise so far as my own observation extends. And I am fully convinced that if I have ever seen Christianity in the world, and the Spirit of Christ, it has been exhibited by those, as a general rule, who have professed to believe and to have received this doctrine of entire sanctification into their hearts.

9. How amazingly important it is that the ministry and the Church should come fully to a right understanding and embracing of this doctrine. It will be like life from the dead! The proclamation of it is now regarded by multitudes as "good tidings of great joy." From every quarter, we get the encouraging news that souls are entering into the deep rest and peace of the gospel, that they are awaking to a life of faith and love—and that instead of sinking down into Antinomianism, they are eminently more benevolent, active, holy, and useful than ever before—that they are eminently more prayerful, watchful, diligent, meek, sober-minded and heavenly in all their lives. This, as a matter of fact, is the character of those, to a very great extent at least, with whom I have been acquainted, who have embraced this doctrine. I say this for no other reason than to relieve the anxieties of those who have heard very strange reports, and whose honest fears have been awakened in regard to the tendency of this doctrine.

10. Much effort has been taken to demonstrate that our views of this subject are wrong. But in all the arguing to this end up till now, there has been one outstanding defect. None of the opponents of this doctrine have yet showed us "a more excellent way and told us what is right." It is certainly impossible to ascertain what is *wrong* on any moral subject unless we have before us the *standard of right*. The mind must certainly be acquainted with the rule of right before it can reasonably pronounce anything wrong, for "by the law is the knowledge of sin." It is therefore certainly absurd for the opponents of the doctrine of entire sanctification in this life to pronounce this doctrine wrong without being able to show us what is right. For what purpose then, do they argue, who insist on this view of the subject as wrong while they do not so much as attempt to tell us what is right? It cannot be pretended that the Scriptures do not teach anything about this subject. And the question is, What do they teach? Until it is definitely ascertained what the Bible does teach, it can by no possibility be shown what is contrary to its teaching.

Therefore, we call upon the denouncers of this doctrine, and we think the demand reasonable, to inform us definitely how holy Christians may be and are expected to be in this life. And it should be distinctly understood that until they bring forward the rule laid down in the Scriptures on this subject, it is but arrogance to pronounce anything wrong. The same principle applies if they should pronounce anything to be sin without comparing it with the standard of right. Until they inform us what the Scriptures do teach, we cannot suppose ourselves obliged to believe that what is taught in this book is wrong or contrary to the language and spirit of inspiration. This is certainly a question that ought not to be thrown by the wayside without being settled. The thing at which we aim is to establish a definite rule or to explain what we suppose to be the real and explicit teachings of the Bible regarding this point. And we do think it absurd that the opponents of this view should attempt to convince us of error without so much as attempting to show what the truth on this subject is. As if we could easily enough decide what is contrary to right, without possessing any knowledge of right. We beseech, therefore, our brethren in discussing this subject to show us what is right. And if this is not the truth, then show us a more excellent way and convince us that we are wrong by showing us what is right. For we have no hope of ever seeing that we are wrong until we can see that something else, other than what is advocated in this discourse, is right.

11. I have by no means given this subject so ample a discussion as I might and should have done, due to my numerous cares and responsibilities. I have been obliged to write in the midst of the excitement and labor of a revival of religion, and do not by any means suppose, either that I have exhausted the subject or so ably defended it as I might have done had I been in other circumstances. But dearly beloved, under the circumstances I have done what I could and thank my Heavenly Father that I have been spared to say so much in defence of the great, leading, central truth of revelation—the *entire sanctification of the Church by the Spirit of Christ.*

And now, blessed and beloved brethren and sisters in the Lord let me beseech you, "by the mercies of God, that ye present your bodies a living sacrifice, holy, acceptable unto God, which is your reasonable service." "And the very God of peace sanctify you wholly; and I pray God your whole spirit and soul and body be preserved blameless unto the coming of our Lord Jesus Christ. Faithful is he that calleth you, who also will do it."

THE OPINIONS OF THE REFORMERS AND OF SUBSEQUENT DIVINES ON THE SUBJECT OF SANCTIFICATION*

By Henry Cowles

Some use may always be made of other men's opinions. Yet he would greatly lack sense who should set out to make all other men's opinions his own, by believing all that has ever been believed. But the man who adopts other men's opinions merely because *they* believe them, does substantially this very thing.

The Reformers were great and good men; and so have been the long line of orthodox theologians from their day to our own. I revere their memory, and love to do them honor. But when called to canvass their opinions and to form my own, I remember that I am to call no man master on the earth; for one is my Master, even Christ. With the Bible in my hand, on the great protestant principle, I am responsible for my own opinions of its meaning. The opinions of learned and able men may aid me in my researches after truth. Yet when I ask the question, What amount of confidence shall I place in their views? I am bound to inquire under what circumstances those views were formed, and especially under what influences resulting from philosophy, from the rest of their theology; and from the prevalent discussions of the day, they were led to adopt such views as they did on the point in question.

1. In this manner I propose now to refer briefly to the opinions of the Reformers and many of their successors on the subject of sanctification, and inquire what degree of confidence ought to be placed in those views *because those great men held them.*

a. It will not be doubted that the Reformers held the doctrine of

---

*From the *Oberlin Evangelist*, April 1, 1840, and continued in the edition of April 22, 1840.

physical innate depravity. I understand them to hold that all sin originates in a fountain lying back of moral action, in the "flesh," as they
often term it. No volition or moral purpose of ours, no consecration of
ourselves to God, can control, or directly affect this flesh. What *remote*
bearing our moral action might have on this fountain of sin does not
clearly appear; but it does appear that, in their view it is not a thing
of volition—is not a voluntary state of either mind or body; but exists
in consequence of our descent from Adam, and continues, despite all
human agency to make it otherwise.

b. Consequently, *they held the doctrine of physical regeneration
and sanctification.* By this is meant that the effects, known as regeneration and sanctification, are wrought, at least in part, upon this
antecedent fountain of corruption. And so far as they are produced,
they are wrought not at all by ourselves, but by the Spirit of God.

c. In regard to the spirituality of the divine law, they held that it
demanded such, and so much love as must be incompatible with loving
any other being at all, and even with our condition in the present
world. Thus Calvin, "The precept of the law is—'Thou shalt love the
Lord thy God with all thy heart.' That this command may be fulfilled,
we must be previously divest of every other perception and thought—
our heart must be free from all desires; and our might must be collected
and contracted to this one point. Those who, compared with others,
have made a very considerable progress in the way of the Lord, are
yet at an immense distance from this perfection." With these given
premises, his inference follows most conclusively.

d. As the natural result of this view, they maintained that however
much Christians may strive to obey, they never yet do obey the law
perfectly in any single point or act whatever.

e. They also said perfect obedience is rendered impossible by our
connection with the flesh, and always will be impossible while we are
in the body. In the words of Augustine and Calvin: "Since the highest
excellence in this life is nothing more than a progress toward perfection, we shall never attain it till, being divested at once of mortality
and sin, we shall fully adhere to the Lord."

f. They also held that remaining sins are *profitable* to the Christian. Luther also taught, "that it is very profitable to feel the unclean
lusts of the flesh," because it keeps us humble; that it profits us very
much to feel sometimes the wickedness of our nature and the corruption of our flesh, that by this means we may be waked and stirred up
to call upon Christ; and that "these remains of unclean lusts and sins
do not at all hinder, but greatly further the Godly."

g. They maintain without scruple that God demands more than
we can perform, and that they are in great error who suppose that God
measures our duty by our ability. See Calvin on 1 Thess. 5:23.

h. The difficult question of how can we be justified and accepted of
God *while actually violating His law,* Calvin met by cutting the knot

at once, and maintained that believers are not under the law, and are not to be judged by that rule. Thus he says, "Their consciences do not observe the law as being under any legal obligation; but, being liberated from the yoke of the law, they yield a voluntary obedience to the will of God." "Although you do not yet experience sin to be destroyed, and righteousness living in you in perfection, yet you have no cause for terror and dejection of mind, as if God were perpetually offended on account of your remaining sin, because by grace ye are emancipated from the law that your works may not be judged according to that rule." This development of Antinomianism has filled me with amazement. It is a striking instance of one error naturally producing another.

I only add that the great point of controversy between the Reformers and the Papists all along, was justification by faith, as opposed to justification in part or wholly by good works. Hence their minds were not brought to bear directly upon the questions, How much, and in what way the Christian may be sanctified in the present life? Yet incidently, their views on these points are brought out with sufficient fullness.

2. The views of the Reformers have had immense sway over the Protestant world down to our own day. Every inch of ground gained in improving their views, even of the philosophy of doctrines, has been strenuously contested. Of course, it is not strange that on many or most of the points mentioned above, the mass of subsequent theologians have held with the Reformers. But we will briefly specify. They have generally held:

a. Sanctification is progressive and never perfect till death.

b. No man can obey the law perfectly in any one instance. Thus the Larger Catechism of the Presbyterian Church holds, "that no man is able, neither of himself, or by any grace received in this life, perfectly to keep the commandments of God, but doth daily break them in thought, word, and deed."

c. The sinful cause of all sin lies back of voluntary action. They have, however, more generally placed it in something called relish, taste, or disposition; concerning which some have maintained that it is, and others that it is not, a voluntary state of mind, and subject to the control of the will.

d. Some of them have maintained that God's explicit purpose and wish is to have His people sanctified only in part during this life. He might sanctify them wholly, but deems it best on the whole to sanctify them only in part. Their sins will be more for His glory than entire holiness could be.

e. Again they have held such views of the state of sinless perfection, as must of course preclude the possibility of attaining it in this life. Thus Andrew Fuller writes, "The disparity between the highest degree of holiness (on earth) and a state of sinless perfection, is inconceivable." "For the Church of God, in full remembrance of its foul roots, to feel itself 'holy and without blemish,' is an idea too great for sinful creatures to comprehend."

f. Their minds do not seem to have been turned very directly to the power of faith in Christ as the grand moral influence which sanctifies the soul, and gives abiding victory over sin. They do not seem to have contemplated very directly whether the grace of Christ through the Spirit is such, and may be so received, as to keep the soul in a state of constant obedience to the known will of God, and give constant victory over all temptation.

3. Having now the history of the doctrine before us, we are prepared for the great question: What amount of confidence ought to be placed in these opinions, considering the circumstances under which they were formed, the philosophy and theology with which they were formed, the philosophy and theology with which they stand connected, and the amount of candid discussion which the vital points of the subject have ever received? Obviously, this confidence ought to be modified in view of the following facts and considerations.

a. They were formed under the influence of sturdy opposition against extreme errors. Against the false doctrines of the Roman church, they waged endless and desperate war. The Papists really paralyzed the influence of the divine law—that is, regarded a multitude of things which are flagrantly sinful to be no sin at all—and held utterly false and ruinous views of good works, expecting acceptance with God and pardon for past sins. They expected this, in part at least, on this ground—They "dreamed," says Luther, "that holy men have the Holy Ghost in such sort, that they never have or feel any temptation," and are "vaunted of their holiness as if they had never committed any evil."

Against these views, the Reformers rightly judged it their duty to contend boldly. But they were only men, and therefore were not beyond the danger of being pushed over into extremes, opposite to those against which they contended. I do not maintain that the fact of their opposing one extreme error proves that they fell into an opposite one; but I may with deference suggest whether views formed under such influences of strong opposition against extreme error, are worthy of unabated confidence. Do the known laws of the human mind authorize it?

Yet their views must stand ultimately on their own merit. There would I let them stand. When, however, I see them maintaining staunchly, that God's law demands vastly more of man than he can possibly do in a single point, I cannot help asking how they came to adopt such an opinion; and the history of its origin helps me to estimate the confidence which is its rightful due.

It is also worthy of serious consideration that Germany was long the seat of successive forms of fanaticism and its attendant errors. In earlier times, the Freer spiritual orders, and in later times the Anabaptists, held notions subversive to the law of God. Of these, some of the former class maintained that "the soul when absorbed in the love of God is free from all law, and may gratify every natural propensity without guilt; that perfect virtue and perfect beatitude may be obtained in this world; that the mind should be called away from the external and sensible parts of religion and fixed on inward and spiritual worship; and then is removed above every worldly consideration so that the moral virtues, as well as religious ceremonies may be neglected without offense." This doctrine was closely allied to the mystical notions about a reunion of the soul with God, from whom it is supposed to have emanated. It should be remembered that these errors lay directly under the eye of the Reformers, and could scarcely fail to modify their own views of the points here involved.

b. Their views were formed under the influence of a most defective system of philosophy. I refer to their philosophical views of the causes or origin of sin. Now if it were true that sin is in us, antecedently to any moral action, and will remain there as long as we are in the flesh, despite all we can do, and all God can help us do, then indeed would their views of sanctification be sound to the core. The great question is settled forever. Do what we may, there is no abiding and universal victory over the world and sin. It is easy to see that this philosophy demands this theology, and doubtless had no small influence in giving it birth. It lies legitimately at its foundation. If the foundation be rotten, will the superstructure stand?

On the other hand, suppose that there is no sin except in moral action, that under God's renewing and sanctifying grace the soul of man may turn heartily and utterly against all sin— that sinful habits may be reversed, artificial lusts subdued and slain, and our constitutional appetites and propensities be so sanctified as to become occasions of holiness rather than of sin—then is not the state of the case materially changed? If the latter views are true in philosophy, in revelation, and in fact, is not the way open for a different system of views in regard to sanctification from that held by the Reformers?

c. By many, not by all, the doctrine has been maintained that God justly may, and actually does, demand of His creatures what they are in every sense unable to perform. That this sentiment is false, I shall not deem it necessary to show now by any extended argument. I only say that it is very obviously unjust, and therefore cannot be true of a just God. Also, the very terms of the law repudiate the position utterly: for the law, as given in epitome by Christ, demands only that we "love the Lord with all the heart, soul, mind, and strength"—nothing more.

It is easy to see the effect of such a sentiment on the question of attaining holiness in this life. If the moral law is the standard of obedience, as all admit, and if this moral law undeniably demands more than we can possibly perform, then perfect obedience is, of course, out of the question.

On this point, I have only two suggestions to make. First, the premises are that God's law demands more than men of themselves, or by any grace, can in this life possibly perform: the conclusion is, that no Christian can in this life attain complete victory over sin. Now if the premises are false, is not the conclusion, certainly insofar as it rested on those premises, at least *doubtful*?

Second, the doctrine that God demands more than we can do, even with all the grace He will give us, has had some kind of influence on the Church. I ask if it has not been utterly and terribly Antinomian? If it has not crushed the aspirations of the renewed soul after holiness—quieted millions of consciences in continued sin, and reigning lust—in short, it has done the very same thing in regard to the onward and high attainments of the Christian which the doctrine "you can't repent if you try" has done to keep men from repenting. I cannot refrain from suggesting these inquiries to the consideration of those, especially, who manifest particular interest against the evil of Antinomianism. I honor their zeal against that giant evil; will they accept a hint which may aid them in their noble conflict against it?

d. The gift of the Holy Ghost has been regarded as dependent upon divine sovereignty. This consideration naturally and almost unavoidably depreciates our own views of the infinite freeness of grace with which it is promised, and greatly diminishes our sense of personal responsibility to obey the command, "Be ye filled with the Spirit."

Under the influence of this view of God's sovereignty in bestowing His Spirit, who has felt bound to be holy like Paul? Who has believed that he not only ought to be, but actually *might always be* "filled with the Spirit"? Who has appreciated the promise which bids us "ask and we shall receive"? God is more willing to give His Holy Spirit to those who ask, than any of you who is a father is willing to give bread to his starving child. Has not this great and rich promise been virtually frittered away?

And here I ask further, can such a view of God's dispensation of His Spirit be the gospel of Christ Jesus? If it is true the Holy Spirit is promised and given with the great generosity of a God—that of Christ's "fullness we may all receive"—that "having these promises," that is, of an indwelling Spirit we may hope to "cleanse ourselves from all filthiness of the flesh and spirit, perfecting holiness in the fear of God"; then could it not follow that Christians not only ought to, but actually may, and sometimes do, "abide in Christ"—"walk in love"—"be filled with the Spirit"—"keep a conscience void of offense"—live "dead to the world, and alive to God through Jesus Christ"?

While men suppose the gift of the Spirit to be in such a sense sovereign as to have no connection with our faith, prayer, or efforts of any sort, and so scanty as not to aid the Christian to obey the law fully in any one instance, is it strange they should believe entire consecration to God impossible; or, their premises being false, need to surprise us if their conclusion should be false also?

All the Reformers, and very many subsequent orthodox theologians, have maintained that sin in the Christian is *profitable to him, and greatly beneficial on the whole.* In response to this sentiment, I ask: Then why not have *more* sin, even as much as any Christian may choose to commit? Why not, the more, the better? Why should God send His Son "to turn away every one from his iniquities," and His Spirit "to sanctify them wholly?" Why not admit sin into heaven to enhance its blessedness and the glory of God? Why does God declare that "this is His will even your sanctification"?

In the final analysis, the doctrine is, "Whatever is, is right;" and where will this lead us? I dare not speculate. I only add that this sentiment cannot be otherwise than dreadfully Antinomian in its tendency. It seriously perverts any system of theology in which it forms an element, and ought to discount largely from our confidence in the truth of all those positions which stand intimately connected with it.

f. The question *how* men may be sanctified, and *how* far they may be in the present life, has never been a general topic of thorough, candid, discussion. At no period have the mind and heart of the Church been generally and powerfully focused on these points. Of course, we cannot be certain where their views would settle if, under the great outpourings of the Spirit of God, such a deep and prayerful investigation were to be made. And of course we cannot rest with so much confidence on the views of the Church, as if these points had been deeply discussed, and especially, as if they had been discussed under peculiarly rich outpourings of the Spirit.

But these points must and will be discussed before the Church can shine forth in the beauties of holiness. May God turn the hearts of His people upon these inquiries with fervent prayer, and quenchless desire for truth; and then may He pour floods of sunlight upon His great promises and glorious provisions for sanctifying His people.

g. The great secret of the gospel's power to save from sin seems to have been very imperfectly understood. Beyond all question, this lies preeminently in the character and work of Christ, made manifest to the soul by the Holy Ghost. "He shall take the things of mine, and shall show them unto you." Then, "beholding as in a glass the glory of the Lord, we are changed into the same image from glory to glory even as by the Spirit of the Lord." Here lies a power, in its nature, adapted to kill the influence of temptation, and sustain in vigor the spirit of obedience; or in the better language of the Bible, to "give the victory over the world," to "change us into the same image from glory to glory"—to "cause us to walk in his statutes," and ever "do all things through Christ who strengthens us."

Now is it very strange that while the meaning of these promises and declarations has been but very imperfectly understood, men should have held very low views of what God, through the gospel, can and may do for the sanctification of His people? Shall we give all credit to their views *because they held them*, when we know the great vital points of the subject were seen by them only "as in a glass darkly?"

To the entire strain of doctrine developed above, there have been some decided exceptions. The reader hardly needs to be reminded of Wesley and his followers who are well known to have held views quite different in most points from the system above given. Also, the writer has credible authority for the fact that there have been Christians in Germany, ever since the Reformation, who have held that the provisions of gospel grace are adequate to meet the needs of believers—that this grace through faith may be received by all, and is received by some—and that when received fully, it *does* give continual victory over the world and temptation. How numerous this class of Christians has been, is not definitely known. It is said also that similar views have long been held in the North of Scotland and by some, at least, among the Quakers. (See Barclay on Perfection.)

It deserves notice and is an encouraging consideration that some have most manifestly attained a state of entire consecration to God, who have renounced and opposed the sentiment (as they understood it) that Christians in this life become sinlessly perfect. In regard to such cases, there is no occasion to contend about the meaning of terms. They may have had such views of sinless perfection as are quoted above from Fuller, or their sentiments in regard to indwelling corruption may have utterly forbidden the idea of exemption from it while in the body. The great question is, Have they attained the real thing? Are they habitually dead to the world and alive unto God? Do they really gain the victory over the world through faith in Jesus Christ? Are their souls wholly drawn out in love to God and love to man? Through infinite grace sustaining them, do they fulfill all their various moral and social duties, and do all for God? In short, is it their meat to do the will of their Father and to finish His work by fully doing all His known will? If so, I would choose to call this state one of entire consecration to God. Some would call it, entire sanctification. And others still prefer the phrase, Christian perfection. We have better work to do than dispute about terms.

The position I now take is that some have held the state now described to be attainable and even to have been actually attained, who yet have altogether disavowed the views supposed to be held under the phrase, sinless perfection. Their testimony is pertinent and the more valuable because they had no favorite doctrine to support, and certainly not the doctrine that grace may sustain in the soul the spirit of holy obedience.

The reader is referred to Pres. Edwards' account of the revival in his day, and especially to his description of "The nature of the work in a particular instance."

Let him notice the individual's *love to Christ.* "The heart was swallowed up in a kind of glow of Christ's love coming down as a constant stream of sweet light, at the same time the soul all flowing out in love to Him, so that there seemed to be a constant flowing and reflowing from heart to heart. The soul dwelt on high, was lost in God, and seemed almost to leave the body." "This heavenly delight has been (not transient, but) enjoyed for years together." "The soul was so strongly drawn toward God and Christ in heaven, that it seemed to the person as though soul and body, would as it were of themselves, of necessity mount up, leave the earth, and ascend thither." "The body often fainted with the love of Christ." Now does not this look like a voluntary consecration of all our powers of affection to God and Christ?

Again, contemplate *her renunciation of the world, and devotion of heart and life to God.* "All that is pleasant and glorious, and all that is terrible in this world, seemed perfectly to vanish into nothing, and nothing to be left but God, in whom the soul was perfectly swallowed up, as in an infinite ocean of blessedness." "There was a daily sensible doing and suffering every thing for God, for a long time, eating, working, sleeping, and bearing pain and trouble for God, and doing all as the service of love, with a continual, uninterrupted cheerfulness, peace and joy."

Here also was *actual victory over sin,* and even those habits of body and mind which sin had caused. This person, under lower degrees of grace had been subject to many infirmities and much unsteadiness; "but strength of grace and divine light wholly conquered these disadvantages, and carried the mind, in a constant manner, quite above all such effects." During the past three years "every thing of that nature seems to be overcome and crushed by the power of faith and trust in God, and resignation to Him."

Again, there was a most faithful, laborious, and cheerful discharge of all the relative social and moral duties. And all this began with intelligent consecration to God. It was accompanied with sweet and deep humility, and with strong, entire dependence on the present grace and help of God through His Spirit.

Whatever we call it, it is a blessed state. She most manifestly maintained the spirit of simple-hearted obedience to God. It was her unwavering, all controlling purpose to do God's will.

This is the state to which I suppose Christians may arrive, and in which they may abide. Would to God the whole Church might awake to know her privilege and her duty as to this attainment. Would to God that she might so believe in the provisions of gospel grace as to lay hold of and to abide in the light, and love and victory of "living by faith on the Son of God."

4. As to the doctrine of physical depravity, the Reformers did not mean to teach that actual sin is not voluntary action. They manifestly meant to carry the conviction home to every man's conscience that all his actual trangressions are really free acts of will and verily guilty. On this point, thus far, no exception is taken against their views. But

in connection with this, they also hold that sin is in man antecedently to any intelligent moral action. They believe the very root and seed of all sin lies back of voluntary action and is the cause why this moral action is what it is—that it is born in us—came from Adam through his fall and corruption, and is a calamity, an evil, which, unaided by God, we cannot remove; and in fact will remove only in such ways, and to such an extent as shall please himself.

Thus Calvin: "The natural depravity which we bring from our mother's womb, though it does not soon produce its effects, is still however, sin in the presence of the Lord, and deserves His punishment." "Corruption was transferred from Adam to us, his descendants." "Adam's sin is the cause of ours. I call it ours because it is natural to us, and we are born with it." "Our nature being corrupted in Adam, is bound under the guilt of iniquity in the sight of God." "The mere participation of human nature is sufficient to entail the wretched inheritance of sin, for it resides in flesh and blood." (Calvin on Romans 5.)

Also: "Original sin is an hereditary depravity and corruption of our nature, diffused through every part of the soul, which first makes us obnoxious to the wrath of God, and then produces in us those works which the Scriptures denominate the works of the flesh." "Men are ruined not only by the faultiness of a criminal course of conduct, but also by a depravity of nature." "Though infants have not (at birth) produced the fruits of their unrighteousness, yet they have the seed inclosed in them; nay their whole nature is a mere seed of sin, so that it cannot but be odious and abominable to God."

Of man's power to do right, Calvin speaks thus: "The will has not indeed perished, because it is inseparable from the nature of man, but is so chained by depraved lusts that it is not able to aspire to any good thing." "The will is held bound in such a subjection to sin that it is not able to turn—much less, apply itself to that which is good." "Such is the depravity of nature, that it is not possible for him to be excited to any thing but evil." (Calvin's Institutes.)

5. The Reformers maintained in full that the law demands of us more than we can perform. Calvin defends this point: "It has indeed, long been a common opinion, that the faculties of men are co-extensive with the requirements of the divine law, and it has some speciousness, but it proceeds from a total want (lack) of an acquaintance with the law." "Instead of that, it was made far above us that it might produce a conviction of our impotence." "God requires what we cannot perform in order that we may know what we ought to seek from Him." Institutes. Book 2. Chapter 5:6, 7, 10. "Doth not God then do injustice to man by requiring from him in his law that which he cannot perform? NOT AT ALL." Catechism of the Reformed Dutch Church.

a. The views of original sin and depravity given above, of necessity lead to physical regeneration and sanctification. It will easily be seen that according to this system, sin being in us antecendently to our own agency, and abiding there beyond our power to remove it, three things must necessarily follow.

First our own sin is so far beyond our control, that at the utmost it cannot depend much on ourselves how far we shall be sanctified, or whether we shall be so at all.

Second, regeneration and sanctification are in such a manner the work of God, that if it is also believed that God does not wish or intend to sanctify His people except very imperfectly in this life, something like a paralysis is given to all efforts for eminent, and much more, entire sanctification.

Third, no Christian can know how much he is sanctified. He may indeed be conscious of all his moral acts, and can compare them with the law of God; but his consciousness can take no cognizance of that something which lies back of all moral action, the root and seed of all sin. If it is said that that is known by its fruits, it may still be replied that a temporary suspension of its sinful products may deceive us and baffle all our scrutiny.

b. The reader may be curious to know the practical influence of such theoretical views. I will cite two cases, the first from the experience of Luther, the other from the divinity of Dr. Hopkins of Newport; the first, of the ancient; the last, of the more modern school of Theology.

Luther, commenting on Galatians 5:17, and having shown that in his view, the flesh must be expected always to resist and hinder, adds, "It is very profitable for the godly to know this, and to bear it well in mind, for it wonderfully comforteth them when they are tempted. When I was a monk, I thought by and by that I was utterly cast away if at any time I felt the lusts of the flesh; that is to say, if I felt any evil motion of fleshly lust, wrath, hatred, or envy against any brother. I essayed many ways to quiet my conscience; but it would not be, for the concupiscence and lusts of my flesh did always return; so that I could not rest, but was continually vexed with the thought that I had committed this or that sin. If I had then rightly understood these words of Paul, I should not have so miserably tormented myself; but should have thought and said to myself as now I commonly do; Martin, thou shalt not utterly be without sin, for thou hast flesh; thou shalt therefore feel the battle thereof according to that saying of Paul, 'The flesh resisteth the Spirit.' Despair not therefore, but resist it strongly, and fulfill not the lusts thereof. Thus doing thou art not under the law." Again, "Christians know that the remnant of sin which is in their flesh is not laid to their charge, but is freely pardoned. Although they feel the flesh to rage and rebel against the Spirit, and themselves also do sometimes fall into sin through infirmity, yet are they not discouraged, nor think therefore that their state and kind of life, and the works which are done according to their calling displease God." (Luther's Works, I. 321,2.)

The reader will not fail to notice here, the comfort obtained while in sin. Some sin of a certain kind is not laid to our charge, but freely pardoned, even while *in us*. And falling into sin sometimes through infirmity does not displease God. Alas! such fruits of such theology!

The views of Hopkins may be given in these quotes. He held that "it is made certain by a divine constitution that no man shall be without sin in this life"; "that God has determined and made it known that no man shall live in the body without sin." In view of these premises, he formally discusses the question "whether Christians ought to pray that they may be perfectly holy in this life?" and answers it most decidedly in the negative. He admits indeed that it is "possible for a Christian to have such a clear view of his own sinfulness, of the evil of sin and its hatefulness, of the desirableness of being delivered from it and of being perfectly holy and conformed to Christ, as earnestly to pray that if it be consistent with the will of God, he may be freed from all sin, and live a perfect holy life for time to come; not at that time remembering that God has revealed that no man shall be so in this life"; and closes by saying, *"PERHAPS this is not sinful"*! It being a mere mistake into which a Christian may fall through the ardor of his hungering after righteousness, it may possibly be no sin!

This doctrine of Dr. Hopkins, however fair in theory, and apparently strong in argument, is radically defective for practice, unless accompanied with full instructions on at least the two following points, which the Dr. seems to have omitted.

First, he should have told us definitely how much sin we must have, and therefore may indulge, and how great that amount is from which we must not even ask for deliverance. Without instruction on this point, how shall I dare to pray for any degree of sanctification? Who can tell me how soon I shall step over the unknown line, and my very praying for holiness become sin!

Second, he ought to have informed us whether, since we may come boldly and ask for grace to help in every time of need, we may with propriety ask God to help us bear as well as we can with that amount of sin in us which His divine constitution has determined that we shall always have on earth. I know not a more crushing evil than the necessity (if it be one) of being my life long a slave to any one however small. Now, may I look up to Jesus, that most compassionate High Priest, and pray for sympathy and help to be as resigned and quiet as possible in the commission of that needful sin? As if Jesus might also help me to be happy in sinning! But my own soul is shocked unutterably with the thought, and I can hardly forgive myself the apparent impiety of even naming it. Yet if the doctrine of Hopkins is true, every Christian who strives after holiness is thrown into this very dilemma.

The premises from which such conclusions legitimately follow must be absolutely false. The Dr. must either have misinterpreted his texts, or have misinferred his doctrine from them. That cannot be Bible truth which overthrows the gospel scheme of salvation from sin, and chills the aspirations of the soul after holiness.

In view of the sentiments now quoted and their manifold influences on the piety of the Church, I remark:

It is no wonder that so few have made high attainments in holiness. In this world of sin and temptation it will always be hard enough, at best, to subdue sin and become holy. These difficulties greatly accummulate when I am forbidden to pray for entire deliverance from sin—encouraged to hope for God's favor while sinning—crushed with the doctrine that the demands of the law are absolutely greater than I can in any way fulfill—instructed that sin is *in my nature* where no efforts of mine can remove it, and finally, that though God could remove it all, yet in His sovereignty, He has determined and revealed it, that He will not remove it all in this life, but will leave some, (how much none can tell) as long as I live.

Is this the gospel—the glorious gospel of the blessed God "which brings life and immortality to light"? Is it the gospel of Jesus, who came to save His people from their sins; who gave us promises that we might "cleanse ourselves from all filthiness of the flesh and of the spirit, perfecting holiness in the fear of God?" Does it agree with his teaching who says, "This is the will of God, even your sanctification?"

It is unutterably grevious that the theology of the Church should be so shaped and held as to retard rather than to promote the sanctification of God's people. There is a great need to hold forth the glorious provisions of gospel grace, to show the power of faith in Christ, and the wonderful adaptation of the Spirit's work to meet our needs. But when these truths are neglected, or worse still, substantially nullified, and the strain of theological teaching is such as has been developed in this article, how woeful are the results! How greatly is the design of revealed truth misunderstood and counteracted! What a contrast between the current teachings and influence of such theology and those of the Bible!

THE DOCTRINE OF SANCTIFICATION AT OBERLIN*

by James H. Fairchild

The theological views of Rev. John J. Shipherd and his associates, the original founders of Oberlin, were in no sense peculiar. These men were all from Congregational and Presbyterian Churches, holding the type of doctrine known as New School Views; and these views they exhibited in a practical form, in the way of aggressive revival movements and measures, rather than in definite dogmatic statements. The doctrine of human ability, however, they distinctly insisted on, and held the sinner responsible for his own conversion or regeneration, under the provisions of the gospel. Mr. Shipherd himself, and most of the early colonists, had been brought into sympathy with the views of Mr. Finney before they had ever seen or heard him, but they had not, in their own thinking, clearly drawn the line between the Old and the New School doctrine.

After Finney, Mahan, Morgan, and Cowles joined the enterprises, the public instruction and the prevailing sentiment became very decided and pronounced. These men were all earnest preachers of human

*James H. Fairchild was a student of Charles Finney at Oberlin College, and later became a Professor at the college as well as President. He condensed and edited for publication Finney's *Autobiography* and *Systematic Theology*, following Finney's death. This article was originally a "paper read at Oberlin before the Theological Institute, July 29, 1875," and later published in *The Congregational Quarterly*, April 1876, pp. 237-259. Since Charles Finney completed his last course of theological lectures on Pastoral Theology at Oberlin in July of 1875, it is entirely possible that he heard this lecture prior to its publication: Finney died on August 16, 1875. I am indebted to Gordon C. Olson for bringing this article to my attention, and for providing me a copy of it for publication in this book.

ability, and of the personal, voluntary responsibility of the sinner for everything about him that can be reckoned as sin. In no other respect did their views differ from those that prevailed in the Congregational and Presbyterian churches of the land. They were aggressive and earnest men, accustomed to aim at immediate and definite results in their preaching.

The preaching of Mr. Finney through the larger towns of New York, and to some extent of New England, and in the cities of New York, Philadelphia, and Boston, had moved the public mind as no other preaching had done for a generation. From the midst of this great movement he came to Oberlin, a community of a few hundred people, mostly of one heart and one mind, gathered for the very purpose of learning and doing the will of God. Preachers and people were still warm from the great revival movement of those times, and impressed with the idea, often expressed, that the millennium was about to dawn. They believed that the "revival state," as it was called, was the normal state of the church, and that the absence of the intensity of experience which characterizes the revival was evidence of backsliding and worldliness.

In the year 1835, Prof. Finney began his work here, sustained by Pres. Mahan and the other professors. The field for the expenditure of this immense personal power and energy was very limited, and the legitimate result was an intense religious activity within this narrow sphere. The anti-slavery conflict naturally absorbed a part of the energy, and the daily work of study and of outward progress in the school and in the community was pushed on with zeal; but the outward and material movements could not satisfy those whose souls were on fire with zeal for the honor of God and the salvation of men from sin. There was only a sinner here and there to be converted; hence the religious activity naturally took the direction of the elevation of the standard of religious experience. Higher attainments and a more entire consecration were urged and enforced. Christians were set upon the work of self-examination, of testing their Christian hope; and it was not a rare thing for a large portion of the congregation, after a searching sermon by Prof. Finney or Pres. Mahan, to rise up in acknowledgment that they had reason to apprehend that they were deceived as to their Christian character, and to express their determination not to rest until their feet were established upon the Rock.

In all this, no intimation was given that it was the privilege of believers to put away sin entirely in this present life. No such hope or expectation was encouraged. Prof. Finney, on one occasion, stated publicly that he would go a hundred miles upon his hands and knees to see a man who lived without sin. The first practical discussion of the question of such a possible attainment occurred in the summer of 1836, in a meeting of a missionary society composed of a few young men who had expressed a purpose to enter upon foreign missionary service, and who held a weekly meeting in furtherance of their spiritual preparation for the work.

The views of the Antinomian Perfectionists, published at New Haven, Conn., in a periodical called *The Perfectionist*, had served to raise the question of obligation as to the degree of holiness which Christians might attain. Although these views, in general, were intelligently and earnestly rejected by the young men, they discussed the question in the light of the New School theology, which they had fully embraced, and reasoned that as all sin is voluntary and inexcusable, a dutiful obedience to God requires its utter rejection, and that the aim and purpose of the believer should be to present an entire obedience. The question was not discussed in a theoretical way, but in earnest application of the principles to present duty, and with much prayer. The young men had the apprehension that they could hope for no further progress in the Christian life unless they were ready to come up to the convictions of present duty. This had been enforced from the pulpit with irresistible logic and power, in the illustration of such texts as this, "He that turneth away his ear from hearing the law, even his prayer shall be abomination"; and does not the law most clearly require abstinence from all sin? Are we not taught that God's "commandments are not grievous"? Does not the Psalmist say, "I have sworn and I will perform it that I will keep thy righteous judgments"?

With such reasonings as these, a few young men, each in a solemn prayer, entered into covenant to do the will of God with all the heart. They contemplated the step as an advance upon their previous consecration, and went forward with solemn earnestness to the work. They quietly announced their purpose among their friends, but made no profession of any attainment. Indeed, they did not look upon the matter as an attainment which was to distinguish them from other Christians, but simply as an attempt to do what it was their duty to do. Their undertaking was generally regarded with disapproval, but as they never afterward alluded to the subject, either publicly or in their own meetings, it soon ceased to excite remark, and was generally forgotten.

In the autumn of the same year the entire community of citizens and students was moved in a religious revival, and one of the most pressing inquiries before the minds of the people was how to overcome temptation and to become established in the Christian life. On one occasion, after a sermon enforcing the duty of a higher consecration, a young man arose and inquired with solemn earnestness to what extent he might hope to overcome temptation, and how far he could trust the Savior for help in his hour of need. Could he ask Him to give a complete victory, or must he expect to go on stumbling as he had hitherto done?

No one dared to tell him that he must not expect too much or that the Savior had not promised to supply every need. Pres. Mahan especially was profoundly moved by the inquiry, and gave himself to prayer until he apprehended, as he thought, the fullness of the love of Christ, in an experience to which he still looks back as the turning point in his Christian life, the hour when he was brought out of darkness into God's marvelous light. The view of Christ as our "wisdom, righteousness, sanctification, and redemption," and the joyful resulting experience, became the theme of the preaching from that time onward, and the idea gained strength that there was a special experience which was the privilege of every Christian to attain, which stood in marked contrast with the previous Christian life—an experience of joy and freedom and peace and stability, over against the former darkness and constraint and stumbling. All the leading ministers seemed to enter into this joyful experience with a sense of release.

The experience was called by different names. A frequent term used was "the blessing," indicating a view of it as a gift rather than an attainment. Some adopted the language of Wesley and called it the experience of "perfect love." This was a favorite term with Pres. Mahan, and the first little volume which he published on the subject was entitled *Christian Perfection*. Prof. Finney preferred the term "sanctification," and commonly employed this in his writings. Prof. Morgan found that the Scriptures referred such an experience to the gift of the Holy Spirit, and his essay on the subject, published in the *Oberlin Quarterly*, was entitled *The Gift of the Holy Ghost*. Prof. Cowles wrote a series of articles in the *Oberlin Evangelist,* afterward gathered into a small volume entitled *The Holiness of Christians in the Present Life.*[1] The idea was much the same under these varying forms of expression, namely, that there is an experience attainable in the Christian life, subsequent in general to conversion, in which the believer rises to a higher plane, secures new views of Christ and His salvation, obtains victory over weaknesses which had before marred his character, and attains a stability to which he was a stranger before.

This experience was presented as an object of pursuit, for the attainment of which special provision is made in the Gospel, and abundant promises are offered. The "new covenant" was, in this view, especially contrasted with the old, as an arrangement for securing the full sanctification of the believer, promising to put the law into the mind and write it on the heart, thus securing to him the obedience required by the old covenant. There was little said about *sinlessness* in connection with this experience. Perhaps Pres. Mahan was less cautious than others in this respect, and sometimes gave the impression that it was his privilege and duty to testify that under this new experience he was free from the consciousness of sin. Others occupying

---

[1]Charles Finney used this same title for a series of sermons first published in the *Oberlin Evangelist* in 1843. This series is now published in the book *Principles of Holiness* (Minneapolis: Bethany House Publishers, 1984).

public positions carefully refrained from such expressions; and confession of sin was, as before, an element in public prayer. Still less was said about *perfection*. Most of the professors avoided the word as liable to convey a false idea, and as utterly inappropriate to their sense of weakness and unworthiness, and of the vast range of experience beyond, which they had not yet traversed. They claimed that they had only begun to test the fullness there is in Christ, and were pressing on in faith and expectation. Pres. Mahan did not differ from others in his view of the state attained in this respect, and was careful to define the term "perfection" as implying merely completeness of trust and entireness of consecration, a voluntary state wholly acceptable to God, leaving still imperfection of view, errors of judgment, and liability to temptation—such liability as existed in the case of the angels and of our first parents, and even in the case of the Savior himself.

Pres. Mahan, more distinctly than others, insisted that this experience produced a "sanctification of the sensibility", and claimed such a result in his own case. He testified that infirmities and passions which had once held him in bondage were slain, and that former temptations, which had appealed to these tendencies and infirmities, had lost their power; that he could stand in the presence of disturbing forces which had formerly overcome him without the slightest perturbation. This subjugation of the propensities he conceived as being a part of the promise of the new covenant—"A new heart will I give you and a new spirit will I put within you, and I will take away the stony heart out of your flesh and I will give you a heart of flesh." In his work, *Out of Darkness into Light,* he says, "Under our renovated propensities and new dispositions, tendencies, and tempers, or 'divine nature,' it becomes just as easy and natural for us to bear the fruits of the Spirit as it was under our old ones to work 'the works of the flesh.' "

This view of the sanctification of the sensibility was rather characteristic of the teaching of Pres. Mahan. According to him, it seemed to involve a supernatural and almost mechanical action upon our human nature, restoring it to its normal state before the fall—all, however, in response to our faith. Pres. Finney, while not disclaiming this idea entirely, and sometimes presenting facts and experiences which were in harmony with it, insisted more on the moral power of Gospel truth on the believer's heart. He found deliverance from temptation and from the power of sin in the views which the Spirit gives of Christ.[2] The truth as it is in Jesus was to him the power of God unto salvation. "Sanctify us through thy truth" was the burden of his prayer and of

---

[2]Charles Finney developed this theme fully in his *Systematic Theology*, but it is omitted from the abridged edition now in print. However, the material may be found in the book *Principles of Union with Christ* (Minneapolis: Bethany House Publishers, 1985).

his teaching; and this was the prevalent idea with the other leaders of thought here.

In connection with this presentation and inculcation of a special experience, the reading of biographies and experiences looking in the same direction was encouraged. The memoirs of James Brainerd Taylor, Hester Ann Rogers, Carvosso, the Wesleys, and the experiences of President and Mrs. Edwards, and other similar works, were read and often referred to in the pulpit. Such experiences became the type or model of the Christian life which was encouraged and approved. Care was taken, indeed, to guard against the idea that we should seek to reproduce such experiences in form. It was generally maintained that each must be led of the Spirit in his own way, and could never exactly walk in the path of another; yet it was inevitable that these special forms of experience should be sought after and cultivated.

The immediate outcome of this movement upon the Christian life here, was undoubtedly a general quickening of the spirituality of believers, and a better apprehension of the Gospel work in delivering from sin and giving the soul power over temptation. A more distinct and higher apprehension of Christ as a Savior from the power of sin, as well as from its penalty, was not only theoretically accepted, but to a great extent practically realized. This was the general result, not merely temporary, but permanent. But beyond this, in many particular cases, a special experience was attained which was accepted as the desired "blessing." Many devoted themselves to its pursuit as the great longing of their souls, and some seemed to attain it. There were remarkable transformations of character in connection with the work, a great release of spiritual power and energy, the effects of which have remained in some cases from that day to this. These persons were generally spoken of as having obtained the blessing, sometimes as having experienced sanctification; and at length, in a limited circle, there developed a tendency to separate believers into two classes, those who had experienced sanctification, and those who were only justified.

At an early day—in 1839 or 1840—a praying circle was organized of those who had attained this special experience, and their meetings were called "band meetings." They were intended to gather only those who had made these special attainments, numbering, as I think, less than a score, that they might counsel and aid each other, and unite their force in the promotion of the work. Occasionally one was invited in who had become especially interested, and was regarded as a seeker of the blessing. The select few felt a greater freedom when gathered by themselves than in the common prayer meeting, and could speak more freely of their experiences. None of the professors belonged to this band, and it was generally understood that they did not think it best to have an exclusive gathering of the kind. It was soon discontinued.

The *Oberlin Evangelist* was established in the interest of these new views in January, 1839, and was published until the autumn of 1862. Its subscription list stood at five thousand for several years, but finally declined, until the paper was suspended for lack of support. The work of those who contributed to its columns was wholly a labor of love. Only the office editor received compensation. The principal writers were Prof. Finney, Pres. Mahan, and Prof. Cowles, and each presented in his own way the new ideas on sanctification.

These views were presented as something new, not in the sense that they were not apostolic and scriptural, but in the sense that they had been lost sight of in the general teachings and experiences of the Church. The Christian community generally received them as something not only new, but as false and mischievous. Thus a discussion arose, and spread far and wide, and warnings and testimonies against error were given by leading men and by presbyteries on the subject of the "Oberlin heresy," and for years it was a question whether the Oberlin church and Oberlin men should have a recognized standing with any religious body in the land. The pressure from without tended to the establishment of an Oberlin sect. This tendency, however, was wisely resisted here. It was thought better to accept for the present mere toleration—and this very sparingly granted—and wait for the future and God's providence to bring a heartier fellowship. That day came at length, either from a change here or abroad, or, as is most probable, from a better understanding on both sides.

It is not my purpose now to follow this discussion in its relation to thought and feeling and action abroad, but to trace the movement in its relation to experience and thought at home. The view presented will embrace matters of fact and judgment, and on some points there naturally will be varying opinions. For the statements offered, no one is to be held responsible but myself.

In the first place, the visible impulse of the movement to a great extent expended itself within the first few years. The special experiences connected with it became less prominent and less sought after. Those who had enjoyed these experiences, especially those whose characters commanded most confidence, seldom alluded to them as peculiar, or as separating them from the great body of Christian people. Their views of the gospel were enriched, and they could speak of a living and present Savior, because they had seen Him and felt His power. Those who went out as preachers, under the impulse of this fresh experience, came at length to see that the old gospel contained their message, and they found it more useful to present the living and present Savior, than to set forth sanctification as a special theory or a special experience. So far as I am informed, not one among them all continued for any length of time to be recognized as a preacher of these special views. They did not repudiate their former views, and have never done so; but they probably found them less divergent than they had supposed from the common faith. They could preach the truth as it is in Jesus more effectively than by giving to their doctrine the odor of Christian perfection, or the higher life. Whatever the motive that operated, the result was as has been stated.

At home, if I have not misapprehended the case, there came to be less confidence in the style of Christian culture involving a special experience, which the movement introduced. It became more and more a matter of doubt whether the seeking of sanctification as a special experience was, on the whole, to be encouraged, and it was not, in general, an occasion of satisfaction when a young man gave himself up to seek "the blessing"; and when he obtained what seemed to him the thing he sought, there came to be less confidence that he had made substantial progress. It was found that such experiences were not always associated with the most stable and mature character. Indeed, if I have rightly observed, it came at length to be the fact, more than at first, that persons of less balanced character were more likely to share in the special experience. It soon appeared, too, that persons who had not partaken of the peculiar experience, in its intense forms, were just as earnest and effective Christian workers in the different departments of Christian labor as those who were supposed to be especially favored.

In the earlier stages of the movement, many persons suffered in their health from the excessive intensity of emotion in connection with their religious exercises. In some cases a lifelong detriment was the result. The feeling at length began to prevail that the idea of a special sanctification induced a religious culture that was too subjective and introspective, and that it was more wholesome to lead the believer out of himself and away from this direct emotional self-culture to the great objects of his faith, the grand facts and truths of the gospel out of which salvation springs. Thus the interest in the movement as to these special forms of experience gradually subsided; and persons who came to Oberlin were heard to remark that they had waited for months and perhaps for years to hear a sermon on the doctrine of sanctification. Those who had watched the movement from the beginning heard sermons on sanctification every Sabbath; but the peculiar forms of presentation were dropped for general purposes, and only at rare intervals were we favored with a sermon on sanctification in proper form.

It was probably true that the preacher felt that the lack of impressibility upon this theme on the part of the people was a mark of spiritual declension, but he instinctively perceived that other forms of presenting the truth were more effective. The day has never returned when our preachers have felt called on to resort to the earlier forms of preaching on the doctrine of sanctification. Not that the preaching has been different in substance—only in form. An occasional sermon on the baptism of the Spirit has been the nearest approach to the earlier type.

Thus far we have witnessed the change in the practical working of the doctrine. Side by side with this change, and conducing to it, there was progress in the formal conception and expression of the doctrine. The earlier view involved the prevalent idea that the ordinary exercises of the regenerate man are in some way defiled by sin—that his holiest exercises need forgiveness, until by death or in some other way he becomes entirely sanctified. The attainment of entire sanctification, therefore, would involve the elimination of this element of sin, and render the Christian entirely acceptable to God in his moral condition.

In the ordinary New School view, the obligation to this attainment must be immediate and pressing, and the ability must exist where the obligation is. The only reason why any believer is not perfectly sanctified is the failure to exercise a perfect faith—of course a voluntary, responsible failure. The way is perfectly open to urge the immediate fulfillment of this human condition of sanctification. Unbelief is the only obstacle, and unbelief is voluntary—a definite sin. This view provides, too, for a clear distinction between the sanctified and the unsanctified Christian. The obedience of the one is complete, of the other partial. The one exercises perfect love, the other imperfect.

Hence, it is to be expected that a remarkable experience will accompany the rising from a partial to a complete obedience, or from an imperfect to a perfect faith and love. It is like a second conversion, and involves the same conditions, repentance and faith. Consequently, there is a natural and obvious ground for a division of Christians into two classes, sanctified and unsanctified. It involves, too, the unscriptural possibility of serving God and mammon, of following Christ while forsaking only a part of what we have; but such a conception is essential to any radical distinction between a sanctified and an unsanctified believer.

In the earlier stages of the special interest on sanctification, the question of the simplicity of moral action was brought forward for discussion. The first and foremost advocates of the doctrine of simplicity were Samuel Cochran and his brother William—the latter afterward professor here—members of the College Class of 1839. The first public presentation of the doctrine here was by William Cochran in an address before the Society of Inquiry in the spring of 1841, and before the Society of Alumni the same year at Commencement. This very able address was published in the *Oberlin Evangelist*, and was very generally accepted here as conclusive on the subject (Second Series.—Vol. VIII. No. 2.). These views were afterward expanded by Prof. Cochran, and published in a series of articles in the *Oberlin Quarterly Review*. The leading instructors and preachers all embraced the view, with the possible exception of Prof. Cowles, and from that day on it became a feature of the Oberlin theology. The doctrine maintains the impossiblility of a divided heart in moral action. The sinner, in his sin, is utterly destitute of righteousness, and the good man, in his obedience, is completely, entirely obedient: sin on the one side and obedience on the other, belonging only to voluntary states. The division of the will between the two contradictory moral attitudes of sin and holiness is a metaphysical impossibility. Such, in a word, is the doctrine, which it is not my purpose to attempt to prove, but to exhibit in its bearing upon the doctrine of sanctification.

One of the most obvious consequences of the doctrine is that conversion is entire consecration; that the earliest obedience of the converted sinner is entire obedience, and that his moral state is entirely approved by God. The very first exercise of faith involves all the faith that under the circumstances is possible, and therefore all that is obligatory. There is no partial faith, in the sense in which faith is a duty, nor, in the same sense, any imperfect love. The sinner in giving his heart to God gives it all, makes no reservations; and holding back corrupts the whole action.

The difficulty with the converted man is *not* that he has "kept back a part of the price," that his obedience is partial while it exists, but that he lacks establishment in righteousness. He is deficient in knowledge of the Savior, of himself, and of the devices of Satan; old habits of thinking and feeling and acting have more or less power with him. Hence he is weak, a babe in Christ, and liable to be overcome by temptation. Therefore his obedience is interrupted by more or less frequent falls, and he must repent and be forgiven and restored—reconverted in the sense in which Peter was "converted" when restored from his sad lapse. He is "weak in faith," not in the sense that there is any voluntary lack in the commitment of the soul to God, but weak in the sense that he has a limited apprehension of the grace and provisions of the gospel, and of the power of Christ to help in every time of need. He accepts Christ for all that he sees Him to be, or he does not accept Him at all. He cannot accept Him as his justification without accepting Him as his sanctification. Indeed, there is no justification without sanctification; and there is no sanctification except "through the faith of Jesus Christ."

The idea, then, of rising from a partial to a complete obedience, from imperfect to perfect faith and love, in the sense in which these are voluntary and responsible acts or states to be required of men, is incompatible with the idea of simplicity of moral action, and hence is not admissible in the Oberlin theology. The work required in Christian progress is growth in grace, enlargement of views, experience of Christ's power and of one's own weakness—all resulting in establishment of Christian character, and more and more complete deliverance from these interruptions of obedience—an obedience more and more constant until it becomes permanent and suffers no interruption.

In this view, every believer is sanctified in the sense that he has utterly renounced sin in his acceptance of Christ, and given Him his whole heart. This is sanctification in the Scripture sense, and all believers are called saints in the Bible, that is, sanctified ones. We hear nothing in the Bible of justified people that are not sanctified. We read, "Whom He did predestinate them He also called, and whom He called them He also justified, and whom He justified them He also '—sanctified'? No, but 'glorified.' " Sanctification is wrapped up in the justification, or rather logically precedes it, and glorification follows. The work of edification which follows conversion is of vast consequence; it is the growth from infancy to manhood. But it can be accomplished by no one act of will, no immediate exercise of faith. There is no promise in God's Word on which a believer can plant himself in present faith, and secure his stability in faith and obedience for all the future, so that we can say of him that he is permanently sanctified. We can say of one that he has grown in the grace of Christ, that he has made attainments in knowledge and experience and stability. We may judge at length, that he is permanently sanctified; but God alone can know. It is not a question of his own consciousness. Consciousness can give the fact of entire consecration, which is the essence of conversion: it cannot give the fact of permanent sanctification; that is in the history of the future, not in present consciousness. Consciousness can never give "a state of permanent sanctification," but only present sanctification; and present sanctification is all that can be required of a Christian. There is no obligation to be permanently sanctified in any other sense than the child is under obligation to become a man. He must hold on his way; and as God gives him time and opportunity, he will grow stronger and stronger. We cannot exhort the believer to, "be permanently sanctified." No such admonition is found in the Scriptures. We are exhorted to endure unto the end, but that cannot be done all at once. We are encouraged "by patient continuance in well-doing" to "seek for glory and honor and immortality," to abide in Christ "as the branch abideth in the vine." This is all that can be done, and it cannot be done by one act of consecration. Consecration is the beginning, and it must be continued to the end.

We find, then, no line of division, on this view of Christian character, between sanctified and unsanctified Christians. All Christians while in the exercise of faith are sanctified, nor is there any clear line between the simply sanctified and the permanently sanctified. The child becomes the man at length, but there is no natural line between childhood and manhood. There are as many different degrees of attainment and establishment in Christian character as there are different individual lives in the church of God.

There are, doubtless, experiences in the Christian life bringing great and apparently sudden releases—such quickenings of the spiritual apprehension, such baptisms of the Spirit of God, as bring in a flood of light; and from that point onward the Christian life may proceed in a higher plane, with a wider view of spiritual things. But we cannot at will secure such experiences. The responsibility of attaining them is not ours, except that we can walk in the highway of holiness along which God arranges these spiritual landscapes. Pilgrim can hold on his way from the City of Destruction to the Celestial City, but it is not for him to determine at what point his narrow path shall lead through the Slough of Despond, or down into the Valley of Humiliation, or over the Delectable Mountains: each comes in its place, and which is best for him he cannot foreknow.

People sometimes speak of these glorious experiences which come after long and patient struggle with trial and temptation as if they were just as much within their reach at the beginning as at the end, and they ought to have seized the blessing at the first rather than the last. No, we might as well look for a harvest without the seed-time. "He that goeth forth and weepeth, bearing precious seed, shall come again with rejoicing." So these heavenly visions, these views from the top of Pisgah, come after years of patient walking with God in the wilderness, and every faithful step brings us nearer. These releases seem sudden. They are sudden in the sense in which, after a toilsome climbing, enveloped by a cloud, to the summit of Mount Washington, upon a lifting of the cloud you finally gaze on the whole mountain region in all its grandeur. Every step of the toilsome climbing brings you nearer to the vision, and the suddenness of the experience is only apparent. So far as a mountain vision is concerned, God might lift us to the summit by His own power in the twinkling of an eye. It is not so clear that He could bring us to the visions of His own glory without prior experiences. There are no spiritual elevators in which men can place themselves at will, and, without an effort, be lifted to the third heaven of holiness; and if we could be thus lifted, who can guarantee that we should be maintained at that dizzy height? God works permanence in holiness in His children through tribulation and patience and experience and hope. The baptism of the Spirit does not set aside this discipline: it works through this the peaceable fruits of righteousness. The day of Pentecost could not come to the world before the Savior's advent, nor to the individual disciple before the years of quiet teaching, the crucifixion, the resurrection, and the tarrying in Jerusalem.

But I must not extend these suggestions. Such facts and views gather about the doctrine of the simplicity of moral action, which took its place in the Oberlin theology side by side with the doctrine of special sanctification already adopted. The incompatibilities soon appeared, and a more or less successful adjustment followed; in some cases complete, in others partial.

Here in our own family, under the roof of our Alma Mater, we may speak with freedom, but with loving reverence, of the labors of those who molded our thoughts and shaped our lives in those days of earnest endeavor and intense experience. A brief allusion to these endeavors will not be received as unkindly criticism, but rather as a grateful recognition of the conscientious fidelity with which our teachers led forward their pupils.

In the writings of Prof. Cowles I do not find evidence that he ever consciously embraced or announced the doctrine of the simplicity of (moral) action. His little work on *The Holiness of Christians in the Present Life*, first published in the *Oberlin Evangelist* in 1839, sets forth, at the outset, what the holiness required of Christians is—a voluntary, abiding consecration of all the powers to the service of God. He makes love, in the sense of benevolence, the fulfilling of the law— just what we can render, nothing more, nothing less. He then considers the point from which the Christian starts in the pursuit of holiness, ascertains where regeneration places him and what are the lowest conditions of discipleship. He says, "There is no room for mistake or question; the doctrine of sincere and full consecration to Christ, as the unalterable condition of discipleship, could not have been made plainer. . . . No man can combine the real service of Christ with the service of sin. . . . Christ will have the whole heart or nothing"; and he adds, "Can this be less than real devotion of the heart, yea, of the whole heart to God? And is it indeed true that real religion can begin with nothing less than entire, yes, *really entire* consecration of our moral being to Christ?" Thus he maintains that the holiness required is rendered in the consecration involved in the first step in the Christian life. He does not so distinctly state that what is required of Christians, beyond this, is to hold on their way, to abide in this consecration, but devotes the remainder of the treatise to showing the provisions made in the gospel for the attainment of holiness, and the encouragement we have for its attainment. Yet he does not speak of any special experience which is to transform the unsanctified into a sanctified believer. The whole bearing of the treatise is to encourage all to Christian fidelity, and to show what helps there are for the performance of Christian duty.

Prof. Morgan distinctly and fully adopted the doctrine of the simplicity of moral action; and his view of sanctification, as presented in his writings, perfectly harmonizes with this doctrine. His published views are contained chiefly in two essays, found in the first volume of the *Oberlin Quarterly Review*, published in 1845. One of these essays deals with the holiness which is acceptable to God, and maintains that it is the doctrine of the Scriptures of the Old Testament and the New. There is no obedience or holiness which does not, for the time, entirely fulfill the requirements of the law; that the first obedience of the new-born soul is love to God with all the heart, and that the obedience of the most mature saint is the same, and nothing more; that such obedience is the condition of all discipleship. "Except a man forsake all that he hath he cannot be my disciple." He shows that all orthodox teaching naturally takes the same form. He quotes to this effect from many writers, especially and abundantly from Pres. Edwards: "They that are God's true servants do give themselves up to His service, and make it as it were their whole work, therein employing their whole

hearts and the chief of their strength. Phil. 3:13. 'This one thing I do.' "
Again, "He that embraces religion for its own sake embraces the whole
of religion."

What is needed according to this view in the case of the converted
man is establishment in righteousness; persistence in obedience. Prof.
Morgan shows, in a second essay, that the baptism of the Spirit is
provided as conducive to this result, and he attributes the transfor-
mation in the case of the apostles, after the day of Pentecost, to the
gift of the Holy Spirit. He teaches that such baptisms are to be looked
for under the gospel dispensation, and all the stability and graces of
the Christian life which result from these. He does not seem to encourage the pursuit of sanctification as a special experience, but does
teach prayer for the bestowment of the Spirit.

Pres. Mahan published his work on *Christian Perfection* in 1839.
This little volume was written under the influence of the generally
accepted view in regard to Christian character. His conception of the
common experience of the Christian was that faith and love and obedience are all imperfect, coming short of the requirements of the law,
and that entire sanctification implies an obedience or consecration
that is both entire and permanent. He seems to assume, although he
does not distinctly state it, that entire obedience will, of course, be
permanent. In maintaining the entire sanctification of Paul against
the objection arising from his dispute with Barnabas, he argues that
even if Paul sinned on that occasion he might have been entirely sanctified afterward. He encourages seeking sanctification as a special experience, and gives his own experience as an illustration.

Soon after this Pres. Mahan accepted and maintained the doctrine
of the simplicity of moral action, and his later writings are intended
to harmonize with the doctrine. In the preface of his last work, published in London, he speaks of the joy and peace and strength which
are the portion of God's people, and says: "If all this is not true of any
believer, it is because he is living below his revealed privileges, and is
thus living because he does not 'know the things which are freely given
to us of God.' It contradicts every true idea of the Christian character
to suppose that a true believer in Christ will walk in darkness, knowing that he may walk in the light; will remain weak, knowing that he
may be girded with everlasting strength; and will continue carnal,
sold under sin, knowing that he may enjoy the glorious liberty of the
sons of God." The volume is largely a record of his own experience,
and he seems to attribute the darkness and depression and stumbling
of his earlier Christian and ministerial life to the fact that he did not
know intellectually what blessings were in the gospel for him. He was
praying and seeking and struggling for years, and at last was delivered
by a revelation to his thought. It was a new conception and not a new
consecration that brought him relief; and he signalized the discovery
by the expression used by Archimedes on a similar occasion, "I have

found it." The result of that new idea was permanent peace and rest and victory from that day on; and all that seems to have been needed for the same attainment long years before was that somebody should have given him this idea. Thus all those years of conflict and of darkness would have been saved. He does not seem to blame himself for that darkness.

The truth probably is that no word of man or of angel, or even the illumination of the Spirit, could have given him the idea. "Tribulation worketh patience, and patience experience, and experience hope." The experience of one soul cannot be imparted to another by any words. Sanctification cannot be put upon a man like a garment; it must be wrought in him by the cooperation of his own will, and in the exercise of all his powers. One can aid another by his suggestions, his sympathy, and his prayers; but he cannot relieve him from the necessity of fighting the battle for himself.

Prof. Finney had published his views on the subject of entire sanctification before he had adopted the idea of the necessary unity of moral action. His first conception of entire sanctification made it an advance from the imperfect or partial faith and obedience attained in conversion, to the complete obedience or entire consecration which the law requires. His original definition of sanctification was entire consecration; and all his arguments on the attainability of sanctification and the methods of attaining it, applied to entire consecration and to that alone.

Before publishing his *Theology*, he had reached the idea of the necessary simplicity of moral action, and he has incorporated this view into his *Theology*, giving the resulting modifications of all the doctrines, but with less success, perhaps, in the case of sanctification than of the other doctrines. The original definition of sanctification as entire consecration cannot stand, because entire consecration is involved in conversion; and every converted person would be entirely sanctified. In defining regeneration he says, "It implies an entire present change of moral character, that is, a change from entire sinfulness to entire holiness" (*Theology*, p. 413.). Of course, then, something beyond entire obedience or consecration must be involved in entire sanctification, if it is an attainment beyond conversion. This fact Prof. Finney accepts, and in his readjusted statement he adds to the definition of sanctification the element of permanence. He says, (p. 595), "Sanctification may be entire in two senses: (1) In the sense of present full obedience, or entire consecration to God; and (2) in the sense of continued, abiding consecration or obedience to God. Entire sanctification, when the terms are used in this sense, consists in being established, confirmed, preserved, continued in a state of sanctification, or of entire consecration to God. In this discussion, then, I shall use the term 'entire sanctification' to designate a state of confirmed and entire consecration of body, soul, and spirit, or of the whole being to God."

By this definition, then, and by the necessity of the case, the entire sanctification, which is to be sought by the believer is *permanent consecration*, and all the argument and instruction upon the subject should correspond with this definition. With this view Mr. Finney begins his treatise on sanctification; but if I read aright, he soon falls back to his former view of sanctification as simply entire consecration, and almost the entire argument applies to that, and to that only.

The Troy Presbytery, in their manifesto on the Oberlin error, had argued that if one should attain sanctification he could not know it. To this Mr. Finney replies (p. 589), "Indeed! Does God command man to do what he cannot know that he does, even if he does it? This would be strange!" He assumes that entire sanctification must be a matter of consciousness. This is true of entire consecration, not of permanent consecration. Nothing but a revelation from God can assure one that he is permanently sanctified. This element of permanence lies beyond the sphere of consciousness. It is true that the Troy Presbytery had confounded entire sanctification with entire consecration, and Mr. Finney's reply might be fair as an *argumentum ad hominem*, but he does not so state it; and afterward maintains at great length that consciousness can testify to entire sanctification. (pp. 750-5) Again he argues (p. 595) that sanctification must be a voluntary condition. But this is true only of entire consecration. The condition of permanence which is to be added to entire consecration is something beyond a voluntary state. All the voluntary action is involved in entire consecration.

Again (p. 599) he says, "It is agreed" that this state must be attained "before the soul can enter heaven." No: conversion, entire consecration only, is the condition of entering heaven. We have no reason to suppose that the penitent thief was sanctified in any other sense.

Again he argues (p. 606) that the law requires a state of entire sanctification. It does not; all that the law requires is entire consecration. It does not require establishment or *permanence* as an immediate duty, any more than it requires the child to become at once a man.

Again he admonishes ministers (p. 614) that they are bound to set up some definite standard of attainment; and to insist upon anything less than entire sanctification is to grant an indulgence to sin. This is true, if entire consecration is sanctification; otherwise not. He who insists upon entire consecration grants no indulgence to sin.

Again (p. 635) he says, "This state is to be attained by faith alone. Let it be forever remembered that without faith it is impossible to please God, and whatsoever is not of faith is sin. Both justification and sanctification are by faith alone." But here we are perplexed. The justified man is in the exercise of faith, and he is not sanctified because he lacks faith, and this lack of faith is sin. This is not in harmony with the doctrine of unity or simplicity of action. It implies a faith or consecration that is less than entire as a condition of justification. The true believer has exercised faith as a condition of justification. What more can he do as a condition of sanctification? If that is all, every true believer is entirely sanctified. Mr. Finney sometimes states that we must receive Christ as our sanctification as well as our justification. But can true faith receive Christ in part, and refuse to receive Him for all that He is known to be? Thus a divided heart or mixed moral action is possible. If it is said that the faith is defective because Christ is not known intellectually as our sanctification, then the ignorance is the difficulty, and that defect of faith is not sin, and knowledge instead of faith becomes the condition of sanctification, as it doubtless is.

In Lecture Sixty-Three Pres. Finney seems to take this view. He considers the temptations to be overcome, and the sources of the motives and forces by which victory is to be attained; and the whole reasoning implies that it is a matter of growth and gradual attainment, and not an instantaneous acquisition by faith. He finds that sin results from an undue development of the sensibility in the direction of appetite and passion, and the remedy is to secure counter-development in the direction of spiritual realities. To this end, he says, knowledge is requisite—knowledge of temptation, its nature and sources; of ourselves, our weaknesses and wants; and above all, a knowledge of Christ in all the various relationships He sustains to His children; and then, in forty-four pages, he sets forth, with wonderful interest and fullness and power, these various relations, numbering sixty-one, which the believer must apprehend in order to maintain his permanent sanctification. The work laid out involves a lifetime, if not an eternity, of study and experience. It is, of course, implied that this knowledge is to be attained under the ministration of the Holy Spirit; but it must be wrought in the believer as a matter of realization and experience, and faith must cooperate at every step in the appropriation of this divine knowledge. The whole conception in this lecture is incompatible with the idea of immediate permanent sanctification by faith alone.[3]

Mr. Finney assumes at almost every step that Christians must be entirely sanctified in this life in order to enter heaven; yet on page 608 he maintains the Old Testament saints did not receive the promises of the New Covenant; that these were reserved for the saints under the gospel; and these promises secure entire sanctification. This argument leads us to apprehend that the Old Testament saints are not to enter heaven, because they were not entirely sanctified.

Thus the careful reader will see that Mr. Finney, in preparing his essay, had not adjusted his views of sanctification to his accepted doctrine as to the nature of moral action, and that the treatise, in almost all its features, belongs to a system of theology maintaining mixed action. Indeed, no other system of theology can provide for immediate

---

[3]*Ibid.*

sanctification as a special experience distinct from conversion, a matter of present obligation to the believer, to be sought and attained at once by faith. Of all theologies now prevailing, the Oberlin theology is least adapted to yield such a doctrine; and so far as this doctrine now prevails among us in limited circles, it is sustained, not by the Oberlin theology or the Oberlin teaching or preaching, but by the writings and periodicals and teachings introduced from abroad, especially of the Wesleyan school.

Pres. Finney's concluding paragraph is full of truth and wisdom, as follows, (p. 765): "But before I close my remarks upon this subject, I must not fail to state what I regard as the present duty of Christians. It is to hold their will in a state of consecration to God, and to lay hold on the promises for the blessing promised in such passages as 1 Thess. v. 23, 24, 'And the very God of peace sanctify you wholly,' etc. This is present duty. Let them wait on the Lord in faith for that cleansing of their being which they need to confirm, strengthen, settle them. All they can do, and all that God requires them to do, is to obey Him from moment to moment, and to lay hold of Him for the blessing of which we have been speaking, and to be assured that God will bring forth the answer in the best time and in the best manner. If you believe, the anointing that abideth will be secured in due time."[4]

This is sound doctrine, in harmony with all present Oberlin theology. It is the theoretical and practical outcome of the Oberlin Doctrine of Sanctification.

James H. Fairchild
Oberlin, Ohio

---

[4]The pages from Finney's *Systematic Theology* Fairchild refers to in this article are from the unabridged edition, now out of print.

Editor's Note: My study of Finney's early sermons indicates that the doctrine of the unity of moral action was strongly implicit. Fairchild's criticism of Finney is set at naught by the chapters in this book from *Views on Sanctification*, where Finney explains why we cannot know consciously if we are "permanently" sanctified. Finney may be confusing in his expressions at times, but I do not believe he is guilty of the errors Fairchild points to when we study him on the whole. The book *Principles of Love* (Bethany House, 1986) should also be consulted in this connection. I believe entire sanctification is loving the Lord our God with all of our heart, mind, soul, and strength; and our neighbor as ourself. This is maintained moment by moment by grace through faith, by the power of the indwelling Holy Spirit, and by our increasing knowledge of Christ as our present, personal, Lord and Savior. We can overcome temptations to sin and selfishness. The Troy Presbytery manifesto with Finney's reply will be found in *Principles of Discipleship* (Bethany House, 1987).

APPENDIX

CONVENTION ON ENTIRE SANCTIFICATION*

"Minutes of the Convention"

Following upon a previous call, a meeting of those interested in the doctrine of entire sanctification in this life was held at Rochester, New York, on the sixth, seventh, and eighth of July, 1841, for the purpose of prayer and consultation in reference to this great subject. The Convention was opened by a sermon from President Mahan on the text, "The Lord is well pleased for his righteousness' sake; He will magnify the law, and make it honorable," (Isaiah 42:21). After a season of prayer, the Convention was organized by the appointment of Rev. A. Sedgwick President, and Rev. H. Lyman, Rev. J. W. Fox, and Rev. L. P. Judson, Secretaries, and a business committee.

The committee made a report which was amended to the following resolution: "That entire sanctification in this life is attainable, in such a sense as to be an object of pursuit with a rational expectation of attaining it." This resolution was fully discussed, and unanimously adopted on the third day of the Convention.

The business committee reported further, and recommended the appointment of a committee to draft a "Declaration of Sentiments," and also a committee to draft a "Circular" to the friends of Zion. After a recess, the committee on the "Declaration of Sentiments" reported. The report was accepted, and the "Declaration," on examination at length, was adopted on the third day and may be found below.

---

*These "Minutes of the Convention" were written for *The Oberlin Evangelist* and published in the August 4, 1841, edition. Included and published with the "Minutes" were the "Postscript to the Minutes of the Convention, by a member," the "Declaration of Sentiments," and the "Circular." The "Declaration" is an excellent summary of the views Finney approved and presents in *Principles of Sanctification*.

In the afternoon of the same day, the committee on the "Circular" reported. Their report was adopted, and may also be found below.

The business committee made a further report recommending the formation of a Society, or the appointment of a committee, to prepare and circulate tracts on the subject of entire sanctification. After discussion, it was resolved to appoint a Committee to write, revise, publish, and circulate tracts in illustration and defense of the doctrine of the entire sanctification of believers in this life. Henry Cowles, C. G. Finney, John Morgan, J. J. Shipherd, and H. C. Taylor, were appointed as said committee.

A subscription was taken up to defray the expense of publishing the minutes of the convention and in aid of the tract cause. Brother Courtland Avery of Rochester, New York, was appointed an agent to receive funds for the tract cause.

A considerable portion of each sitting was spent in prayer, and these seasons were of the deepest interest. The following resolutions were separately offered, discussed, and unanimously adopted:

1. That we recommend to the friends of Zion, who sympathize with us in views on the subject of entire sanctification of believers in this life, to remember the cause in their closets, and constantly to pray for the baptism of the Spirit to rest upon all, *friends* and *opponents*.

2. That we recommend our friends to use all suitable means to secure the reading of publications on this subject.

3. That we also recommend to our friends to hold meetings for mutual consultation and prayer, to secure the cultivation of holiness in their own hearts, and to disseminate the truth in the community.

4. That a standing committee be appointed to confer together on the general interests of the cause of Christian holiness, and that they be empowered to call conventions whenever and wherever the interests of the truth shall in their opinion demand it. The committee members are:

Prof. Upham, of Brunswick, Me.
Alexander N. Dougherty, Newark, N.J.
Fayette Shipherd, Troy, N.Y.
A. Sedgwick, Ogden, N.Y.
M. Tooker, Rochester, N.Y.
J.J. Shipherd, Oberlin, Ohio

The thanks of the Convention were tendered to the Church (the First Methodist Church) whose house they had occupied, and to the citizens, whose hospitality they had enjoyed. The convention then engaged in a most soul subduing and heart melting season of prayer and adjourned.

A. Sedgwick, Pres.

H. Lyman,
J.W. Fox,
L.P. Judson, Secretaries

Postscript to the Minutes of the Convention

by a Member

1. The members of the Convention were mostly from the counties of Western New York.

2. Nearly a hundred enrolled their names, and from two to three hundred were usually in attendance.

3. The meetings were all characterized by the spirit of kindness and brotherly love.

4. The votes were all understood to be unanimous.

5. Antinomian perfectionists, finding in the progress of the discussions that they were not of the Convention, withdrew.

6. Strong prejudices gave place to gratuitous acknowledgments that God was in the Convention of a truth.

7. Frequent seasons of prayer, praise, and conference, which intervened the business sessions, were of a sweetly hallowing character.

8. Sermons by Prof. Finney and Pres. Mahan on the Sabbath preceding and the one succeeding the Convention, and during the intervening week, appeared to be greatly profitable to many of the multitudes who heard them.

9. The closing scene was one of humble, hearty, solemn, joyous consecration to God, rarely witnessed on earth. It was indeed good to be there; for all present who knew God could not but feel, "Surely, God is in this place."

10. The little ones of the Lord returned to their places, comforted and baptized anew for His holy work, and the city left seemed to be a measure in which the leaven of truth was deposited so as to leaven the whole lump.

To God be all the *praise!*

Declaration of Sentiments

On the subject of entire sanctification or consecration to God.

Adopted by the Convention of ministers and others recently held at Rochester.

I. What we understand to be points of agreement between the ministers and members of a great portion of the Christian Church.

1. We agree that entire obedience to the moral law constitutes entire sanctification or obedience to God.

2. We agree that all moral agents are able to render this obedience.

3. We agree that because all moral agents are able to render this obedience, therefore they are bound to do so.

4. We agree therefore that a state of entire sanctification is attainable in this life.

a. On the ground of ability.

b. On the ground of the provisions and proffered grace of the Gospel.

c. That sufficient grace for the actual attainment of this state is abundantly promised in the gospel, and that nothing prevents any Christian from making this attainment in this life but a neglect to avail himself of the proffered grace of Christ.

5. We agree that all are bound to aim at, and pray for, this attainment in this life, and that aiming at this state is indispensable to Christian character.

II. In what we differ.

1. The advocates of this doctrine affirm that obedience to the moral law or a state of entire consecration to God in this life is in such a sense attainable as to be an object of rational pursuit with the *expectation of attaining it.*

2. The opposers of this doctrine affirm,

a. That this state *may* be attained in this life.

b. That therefore it ought to be attained.

c. That we are bound to aim at, and pray for, this attainment in this life.

d. That this state is not attainable in this life in such a sense as to make its attainment an object of rational pursuit, *with the expectation of attaining it.*

e. That it is fatal not to aim at, and pray for, this attainment in this life.

f. But that it is a dangerous error to believe or expect that we shall make this attainment.

III. What the believers in the doctrine of entire consecration to God in this life do not believe.

1. We do not believe that the moral law is or ever can be repealed, or so modified in its claims as to demand any thing less of any moral agent than the entire, universal and constant devotion of his whole being to God.

2. We do not believe that any such state is attainable in this or any other life as to preclude the possibility and necessity of constant growth in holiness.

3. Nor do we believe that any state is attainable in this life that will put the soul beyond a state of warfare with temptation.

4. We do not believe that any such state is attainable in this life as will preclude the necessity of constant dependence upon the grace of our Lord Jesus Christ, and the agency and indwelling of the Holy Spirit.

5. We do not believe that any such state is attainable in this life as to preclude the necessity of much watchfulness and prayer, together with the diligent use of the ordinances of God's house, and of all the appointed means of grace, to perpetuate holiness of heart.

6. We do not believe in any system of quietism [religious mysticism], Antinomianism, or inaction in religion.

7. We do not regard the true question at issue between us to be, whether a state of entire sanctification has ever been attained in this life; but the true question is that which has been stated above, that is: *is this state attainable in such a sense as to render its pursuit, with the expectation of attaining it, rational.*

8. Those of us who have affirmed that this state has been attained, have ever regarded the fact of its attainment only in the light of an argument in proof of its attainability *in the sense above explained.*

9. We have never regarded the proof of actual attainment, either as the great question at issue, or as an argument at all indispensable to the support of the proposition in question.

a. We consider the Bible proof as conclusive in support of the doctrine, without touching the question of actual attainment.

b. If it should be admitted that such a state has never been attained, still we believe the Bible warrants and demands the belief that the Church is destined to make vastly higher attainments on earth than have ever yet been made.

c. If the fact (should it be admitted) that no one has ever attained this state proves that no one ever will attain it; the fact that the world has never been converted, proves equally that it never will be converted.

10. We therefore waive an expression of opinion on the question whether this state has been hitherto attained, lest it should afford an occasion, as it has hitherto done, to divert attention from the great and only fundamental point in debate.

Circular

To all who love our Lord . . . especially to those who are looking to Jesus for present salvation from sin, and the complete redemption of Zion.

We are now constrained by the love of Christ to address you. Having "one Lord, one faith, and one baptism," we speak to you not in behalf of any sect, but in the name of that Head, "whose body the Church is, and of whom we all are members in particular." The truth has made us happily free from desire to proselyte you to any party, and filled us with holy longings to win you entirely and forever to Him, that He may be glorified, the Church blessed, and the world saved through your full redemption.

As sinners saved by grace, we invite you to meet us at the feet of our Divine Teacher (Bible in hand and heart), and hear us about the "great salvation."

That this salvation is great, as the way of escape from the curse of the law, all Christians admit. That salvation from the *penalty* cannot be secured without salvation from the *transgression* of the law is a truth so palpable that it is admitted even by those who preach that all men will be saved. *Present* salvation from sin, the true Church of God has desired most ardently; but not regarding it as attainable, has sunk down desponding, beneath the weeping willows, along the streams of her captivity, instead of uttering the "new song" which deliverance would inspire. But the Bridegroom says, "Daughter of Zion, awake from thy sadness. The Comforter is revealing to His begotten ones the secret of redemption." What this gospel is, as we hold it, you may see in the above *Declaration of Sentiments* of this convention; the substance of which is briefly this:

"Obedience to the moral law, or a state of entire consecration to God in this life, is in such a sense attainable as to be an object of rational pursuit, with the *expectation of attaining it.*"

To argue this proposition does not come within the scope or design of this short epistle. We can only present it as a part of divine revelation to be embraced by simple faith. But, brethren, "if you will do His will, you shall know of the doctrine, whether it be of God." Therefore, in the simplicity of faith, take a few specimens of these glad tidings to us sinners: "He shall save His people *from* their sins." "Who gave himself for our sins, that He might deliver us from this present evil world." "Christ also loved the Church and gave Himself for it, that He might sanctify and cleanse it with the washing of water by the word, that He might present it unto Himself a glorious Church, not having spot, or wrinkle, or any such thing; but that it should be holy and without blemish." "He is able to save unto the uttermost all who come unto God by Him." "Faithful is He that calleth you, who also will do it"; that is, will *sanctify you wholly,* in body, soul, and spirit, and *preserve* you *blameless unto* the coming of our Lord Jesus Christ."

Do you ask, "If Jesus came to bring present salvation from sin, why are not the promises fulfilled in the Church?" We answer, "When the Son of Man has come, He has not found faith on the earth. He has not done many *mighty works* in us, because of our unbelief." We have not attained this great salvation, because "we have sought it by works of the law, and not by faith" (see Romans 9:30-33). In view of such murderous unbelief, we are deeply humbled, grieved, and broken-hearted; and greatly marvel that we should so long have "stumbled at that stumblingstone."

And now, beloved, let us, in much tenderness and strength of love to you as fellow members in our precious Savior, ask you these questions. Why have you departed from Him through an evil heart of unbelief? Why have you "gone astray like lost sheep?" Why have you left the "green pastures and still waters" and "wandered from mountain to hill forgetting your resting place?" Why do you say, "We are delivered to do all these abominations" of unbelief? Jesus "gave himself to deliver *you* from *this present* evil world"; and we know that He does deliver. "You have forsaken the Lord and He has forsaken you; but if you seek Him He will be found of you." "Return unto me, and I will return unto you, saith the Lord." "Look to Jesus," and He will "heal you of your backslidings, and love you freely." "Though you be dead, if you believe in Him you shall live; and if you believe in Him while you live you shall never die." Christ is the true and living way, of present, permanent, perfect righteousness and peace. Look to Him in faith, and He will lead *you* therein. We are exceedingly greived at our former unbelief; but now, through grace, we have great and permanent peace in believing. Dear blood-bought ones, allow us, in kind fidelity to say, we are exceedingly grieved with your unbelief; and were there opportunity, we would fill our mouths with gospel arguments, and urge them with our tears upon your wandering hearts: but we must close our expostulations, beseeching you, by all that is pure and precious in your interests and Zion's, and in those of a perishing world; and in the glory of God our Savior, that you will now heed His soul-subduing entreaty, "Turn, O backsliding children, for I am *married* unto you!"

To you, beloved, who are looking to Jesus for present and permanent sanctification from all sin, we say the following. Settle down at once upon the "exceeding great and precious promises," resting assured that "by these you shall become partakers of the divine nature." Wander not in the wilderness of sin, provoking God by your unbelief, but come straight up to the promised land by simple faith. The substance of this promise is expressed in many other "exceeding great and precious promises." See especially Ezekiel 36:25-37 and Jeremiah 31:31-34 in this context. But references need not be multiplied here. Only receive one of these, "nothing doubting," and you shall be made whole. Do you still feel that you are too weak and simple to fulfill all righteousness? Believe Romans 8:1-4; here it is plain that God in His wondrous grace has made full provision for our weakness and the *fulfillment of the righteousness of the the law in us*; and the context shows that this grace in Christ Jesus is for us even while in the weakness of our bodily state. And forget not that as you obtain righteousness unto *justification*, not by "works of the law," but by *simple faith*, so are you to obtain righteousness unto *sanctification* by faith only: that faith which always *works* to the fulfillment of the law. This faith in our Lord Jesus Christ is connected with the deepest repentance toward God. Christ cannot be thus put on, unless *self* be utterly put off.

Another momentous thought is this: "Yet a *little while* the light is with you; walk while ye have the light, lest darkness come upon you." That is, unhesitatingly pursue the way of this "great salvation," as fast as it is made known to you by the Holy Spirit.

Having thus obtained your freedom, by faith in Jesus Christ—by faith maintain it. "As ye have received Christ, *so* walk ye in Him."

"The life which you now live in the flesh, live by the faith of the Son of God." "*Abide* in Him, and you will not sin." That you may be always, and more and more like Him—look to Him *constantly*. View Him *much* in the glass of His *Word*. *Meditate* much upon His character and life. Draw near to Him in *ceaseless prayer*. Study Him in the memoirs of His saints, as given in the Bible, and the biographies of the holy, connected with different denominations: especially such as Payson near the close of his life, James Brainerd Taylor, Carvosso, Bramwell, Mrs. Hester Ann Rogers, and Mrs. President Jonathan Edwards. Ponder well the living testimonies of those who declare what God has done for their souls. Associate with the spiritual of all classes for the study of the "glorious gospel," conversation and prayer. "Watch unto prayer" always remembering that however "willing the spirit, the flesh is weak." And finally, "wait on the Lord, be of good courage, and He shall strengthen your heart. Wait, we say, upon the Lord." Wait *constantly* on the Lord, and you shall *renew* your strength—yea, you "shall mount up on wings as eagles."

Having the witness of the Spirit and the truth that your fellowship is with the Father, and with His Son Jesus Christ, declare these things to others that they may have fellowship with us; and meekly, charitably, zealously labor to make all men know what is the fellowship of the mystery of free, full, present, and permanent salvation by Jesus Christ, according to His "glorious gospel." Beware that you do not proclaim *your own* goodness, or indulge a thought of it, or even seem to do it. God dwelleth only with the humble and contrite in heart. "Speak evil of no man." If you sympathize with Christ, you cannot but "sigh and cry for the abominations" of unbelief which prevail even in the Church. But avoid a censorious and denunciatory spirit more than you would avoid death. "Love worketh no ill to his neighbor." "Charity suffereth long, and is kind; charity envieth not; charity vaunteth not itself, is not puffed up, doth not behave itself unseemly . . . is not easily provoked, thinketh no evil . . . beareth all things, believeth all things, hopeth all things, endureth all things." Leave not the communion of our Lord's Table, nor in any way make light of the ordinances of His house. Give the right hand of fellowship to all who love our Lord, whatever be their church relations or circumstances. We say not— fellowship error; but fellowship Christianity in whomsoever you find it. Ask none to come over to your church or society, but ask all to meet you in Jesus, and by faith sink with you by baptism into His death, that we all may be one according to His prayer in the seventeenth chapter of John. As a final caution, let us say: beware that you do not "hold the truth in *unrighteousness*." We ask you not to profess this faith, unless by grace you practice it. God calls not for witnesses in word, unless they are themselves "living epistles, known and read of all men."

Finally, beloved, we pray "the Father of our Lord Jesus Christ, of whom the whole family in heaven and earth is named, that He would grant you according to the riches of His glory to be strengthened with might by His Spirit in the inner man; that Christ may dwell in your hearts by faith; that ye, being rooted and grounded in love, may be able to comprehend with all saints what is the breadth, and length, and depth, and height; and to know the love of Christ, which passeth knowledge, that ye might be filled with all the fulness of God. Now unto Him that is able to do exceeding abundantly above all that we ask or think, according to the power that worketh in us, unto Him be glory in the Church by Christ Jesus, throughout all ages, world without end. Amen."

Notice

The following notice of the convention at Rochester is from the *American Citizen*, an excellent miscellaneous and anti-slavery paper published in that city. It is valuable testimony from a man who cannot be accused of prejudice. It is worthy of remark that none of the editors of the religious periodicals, so far as we know, have informed their readers that such a convention was held. Indeed this notice is the only one we have seen in any paper.

"THE RECENT CONVENTION.—A *Declaration of Sentiments* from this body will be seen in another place. With theological *squabbles*, our columns intermeddle not. Facts and occurrences the public, however, wish to be fully apprised of. We were occasionally in the convention, as far as our engagements would permit. There seemed to be the most delightful spirit pervading all its movements. A very full and frank explanation and comparison of views took place. We make no doubt, strong prejudices were vanquished, and that great good was done.

"Two evenings during the session of the convention, Mr. Finney preached in the large Methodist house to large audiences; and again last Sabbath he preached at the same place, morning and evening, to not less than two thousand people. What an admirable God-furnished man, he is! Each discourse contains within itself the germ of an entire system of practical, gospel morality. Commonsense gives a ready assent to each successive proposition. Conscience responds a willing verdict to every appeal. God's revealed truth sustains and enforces the whole. Time fails us: enough for the present."—*Citizen*.